RECOLLECTIONS OF A LUCKNOW VETERAN

RECOLLECTIONS

OF A

LUCKNOW VETERAN

1845-1876

BY

MAJOR-GENERAL J. RUGGLES

GYAN

Published by

GYAN

Gyan Publishing House
5, Ansari Road
Daryaganj, New Delhi-110002
Phone: 011-47034999, 9811692060
E-mail: books@gyanbooks.com

Distribution Network
gyanbooks.com
India, USA, Canada, UK, Australia, France

ISBN: 978-81-212-7107-3 (PB)
First Published, 1906

2nd Impression 2024

Printed at: Gyan Press, Delhi.

RECOLLECTIONS OF A LUCKNOW VETERAN
Author: J. RUGGLES

Anderson—Rajah Man Singh—Desertion of cooks—Further dilapidation of buildings—More of the horizontal mortar—Heavy losses among the Artillery—Effect of an eclipse—Further casualties—The problem of dress and laundry - - - - - - - - - - - - Page 77

CHAPTER VIII.

FURTHER INCIDENTS.

News from Sir James Outram—Welcome sound of artillery—Death of Captain Radcliffe—Flight of the enemy—Arrival of the relieving force—Demonstrations of joy—Losses by the way—Eager enquiries—Delafosse and Thompson among the arrivals—Straitened commissariat—The new tobacco—Lieutenant Moorsom—Death of Neill and Cooper—Details of Havelock's advance—Outram's magnanimity—Recipients of the V.C.—Deaths by sorties—Total losses, European and native—Case of Colonel Birch—Of Graves—Outram in command—Second phase of the siege, the blockade—Successful work by Colonel Napier—Rewards to Ungud and other natives—Discontent of our own men—Unwholesome food—Tantalising position of our stores—Distress and mortality among the wounded—News of the capture of Delhi - - - - Page 86

CHAPTER IX.

ARRIVAL OF RELIEVING FORCE.

Mr. Kavanagh's plucky feat—Casualties from recklessness—Death of Colonel Campbell—Approach of the relieving force observed—Fighting at the Sekundur Bagh—Taking of the Shah Nujeef—Captain Wolseley plants the British ensign—Strength and casualties of Sir Colin Campbell's force—Evacuation of the Residency—My Arab in a palkee-gharry—Terrible experience of Captain Waterman—Removal of the treasury—Our six months' mail—A treasured piece of furniture—Honour for General Havelock—His death—Wisdom of Sir Colin's arrangements—A youthful thief—A novel experience—Arrival at Cawnpore—Kindness of two officers—Irate Mrs. Apthorp—Christmas day—Mrs. Halford again—Reception at Calcutta—Lady Canning's kindness—Ladies of the garrison sail in the *Ava*—Wrecked off Trincomalee—Effect of the calamity—Fifteen months' leave—A strange greeting—Voyage back to India—Thirteen brides to be—Incident at Suez—An exacting charge—"Devils and devils"—An exciting drive - - - - - - - - - - - Page 99

CHAPTER X.

CHINA, 1860-1861.

China in preference to Barrickpore—Work in plenty—Drawbacks of the "irregular" system—The unfamiliar hammock—Visit of Sir Robert Napier—Luxurious voyaging—Hostile Chinamen on the Cochin coast—Singapore—A thank-offering—Drastic measures for drunkenness—The "ripples"—At Kowloon—My friend the compradore—Ordered to Shanghai—A panic-stricken official—Barbarities inflicted on Taipings—An annoying incident—A case of conflicting ancestral strains—From the Stone Bridge to the Ningpo Joss House—Polyglot conversation—A deal in watches—Chinese characteristics—Perilous boating—Pleasant relations with the Legation—Back to India—Penang - - *Page* 113

CHAPTER XI.

INDIA AGAIN.

Arrival at Calcutta—Inspections—Interview with the chief—Ordered to Lucknow—A nocturnal party in strange attire—The tinned sausages—Ordered to Seetapore—Sad memories—Appointed second in command of 19th Punjabees—A night alarm—Mishap with the mess plates—Troops at Morar—Gwalior fort—A mess bungalow secured—Court-martial on a European—Capping stories—Incredulous listeners—An unfortunate addition to the rice—"Kuch Nes"—Tall peas—Sport with Stafford at Mahona—A sensitive spaniel - - - - - - *Page* 124

CHAPTER XII.

BHOOTAN.

Agra and Allyghur—Lucky escapes—Trains in collision—Mr. Barnes at Colgong—Recalcitrant baggage animals—Karajambus—Major Stafford unwell—My little brigade—Cold night work—Harrassed by arrows—Rushing the stockade—The enemy's flag—Commendation from superiors—Leeches—Sad end of the goat—A disastrous march—Agility of cholera patients—Death of Lieutenant Kennedy—Trying climate—At Julpesh—Bamboo houses—Inspection by General Tyler—Stafford rejoins—W—— of "ours"—Renewed operations against the Bhooteahs—Strange use for a telegraph wire—A cork bed and a cork mattress—Monkeys and dogs—Destructive vengeance—Freak of an absentee caterer—Sagacity of an elephant - - - - - - *Page* 133

CHAPTER XIII.

SIMLA.

Return to Allyghur—To Simla on leave—Trip to Narkhunda—Tragic death of Lady Brind—Bobbery Pack at Allyghur—The fatal lampreys—Nynee Tal—The yellow-back out of place—Native sense of humour—Heavy loads carried by women—A bribe for wild coolies—Miscalling of names—In orders for Peshawur—Memorials to General Nicholson—Tame black buck—Earthquake scare at Attock—Cholera precautions upset by frogs—Cholera deaths—A versatile priest—Fruit trade arrested—Suggestion from comparison of cholera poison and snake-bite poison—Strange cases of recovery—Shere Ali—Interesting document possessed by Bahadur Khan—Instances of native prescience - - - *Page* 145

CHAPTER XIV.

TULLA GAON AND CASHMERE.

Khyberees of the Pass—The chowkedar—"Good and faithful servant"—An eccentric chaplain—My house at Tulla Gaon—A zebra hunt—Transposition of place names—Visit to Cashmere—Discomforts of an ekka—The question of pay—A quarrelsome pony—Horns for sale—From Baramulla by boat—The Maharajah's present—Pedlars' wares—A *Shakara*—Shawls and silks—Crows *v.* snake—View from Takht-i-Suliman—Sacred fish at Bawan—Gul Murg—Back to Srinagar—Fishing, but not for ancestors—A shawl manufactory—Charms of the Cashmere valley - - - - - - - - - - *Page* 157

CHAPTER XV.

HOME AGAIN.

Preparations for the lieutenant-governor—Novel footstools—Evening festivities—Back to Baramulla—Modern improvements—A paradise for artists—Return to Tulla Gaon—Disappointment of an enthusiast—In command of the regiment—The Rev. Geo. Maxwell Gordon—An ill-equipped native convert—Right type of missionary for India—The modern carpenter as Christian teacher—Back to Mooltan—A strange coincidence—Greeting by Bomunjee—Brigadier-General MacPherson relieves Brigadier-General Ross—Recollections of twenty-five years earlier—Pay-day—A steeplechase of jackals—Regrets on leaving—Coonorr—Seringapatam—Famous quarters—Colonel Malleson's description of an historic scene—Colonel Scott's house on the Cauvery—Nundydroog—An eerie resting-place—Rats in force—By bullock-cart—Madras—*The Young Cadet*—The titled barber—A pleasant meeting on the *Trinacria*—White-water—Five ways of getting to India—A dream premonition verified—*L'enfant terrible*—Home again—A farewell - - - - - - - - - - - - *Page* 169

CHAPTER I.

EARLY INCIDENTS.

The voyage out—Fellow passengers—A novel flat—A flirtation—Mrs. Grundy—Going for the letters—The result—No money—A good Samaritan—The biter bitten—On active service—Fort Kote Kangra taken—I join Major Abbott's camp—Also my regiment the 41st N. I.

AFTER being two years at Addiscombe, and at the age of eighteen, I left England for India on the 10th of September, 1845, in the ship *Queen*, 1,350 tons, commanded by Captain MacLeod. On going on board at Southampton I was delighted to find that Howell, who had been in my term at Addiscombe, was to share my cabin—for a nicer fellow and more congenial companion there could not be. We had the same tastes: he was fond of drawing, so was I; in fact at the final exam. we were both competitors for the Prize for Military Drawing, but he just beat me-his pen-drawing was perfect.

Travelling in those days was very different from what it is now, and a voyage to India was looked on as a very formidable affair. To me, who had never been away from home, it seemed especially so, and I can well call to mind after sixty years what a wrench the parting was. Up to almost the day of her death my mother told me she never forgot the sight of the train that carried me off as it left Nine Elms Station. The saddest part on these occasions is for those who are left behind. New faces and new scenes soon alleviate and cheer one up.

Among the passengers I recollect was a Mr. Hume, of whom a little story.

In the summer when we went to Southend my grandfather had rooms at the Royal Hotel. There was one waiter there whom he would always have to wait on him; he said he was the most perfect servant he ever came across. Of course I knew the man well and could recollect him for twelve years back. My surprise was great when on board the *Queen* I recognised in Mr. Hume my friend the waiter. He was equally astonished at seeing me; but he told me he was going to join his brothers, who were Calcutta merchants; that in early life he had run away from home and it was only lately he had become reconciled to his family. I went to see him in Calcutta, and found him living in one of the largest houses in Chowringhee!

An incident of our voyage I can now recall, which was rather amusing, although at the time annoying. Howell and I each possessed a filter, and as the allowance of water was limited we found these very useful for storing what we could spare from the daily allowance. One day a missionary, who occupied a cabin opposite to us, asked to be allowed to put some water into our filter; to this request we gave consent; but our vexation was great when we found that he had added sea water under the impression that filters rendered it fresh.

I arrived in Calcutta, after a pleasant voyage, on the 6th of January, 1846. Up to the 10th of February that year (the day on which the battle of Sobraon was fought) I was quartered in the cadet barracks, Fort William; but on that date received orders to join my regiment, 41st Native Infantry, quartered at Noorpore, up in the hills not far from Cashmere territory — a formidable journey as I thought at the time. It was, I believe, about 2,000 miles.

From Calcutta to Allahabad, about 800 miles, had to be performed by water up the Ganges, and I often wonder how many there are now in 1906 who remember this mode of travelling. The railway has of course made the journey shorter, but I am bound to say at the sacrifice of comfort. Being provided by Government with the necessary ticket, on the morning of the 10th I went on board the flat *Soorma* lying at the Ghaut; why called a "flat," I know not; it is simply a large barge with no masts or anything to hamper the deck which is provided with a roof protecting it in all weathers. Below, it is fitted up with roomy cabins, dining saloon, etc., all most comfortable; and large windows, in lieu of port-holes, protected by sunblinds, gave free circulation. In a short time a steam tug, the *Megna*, took us in tow, and we started down the river Hooghly; crossing a short arm of the sea, we entered one of the numerous outlets of the river Ganges which form a perfect net-work of streams called the "Soonderbunds". They are very narrow, giving only just room for the tug and flat; the shore on either side was the densest jungle I ever saw. Tigers, I was told, abounded, and it was not unusual to find in the morning their muddy footprints on the deck, as they used the flat as a bridge to cross from one shore to the other. Every evening the tug stopped at a station to take in wood for the engines, and there we remained for the night, as the channel was too intricate for us to proceed except by day-time. On getting clear of the Soonderbunds we came into the Ganges itself, and here the scenery was very picturesque; and with this mode of travel, to me most novel, it was quite sufficient amusement to watch the fresh scenes that opened out as we proceeded up the river. There were several passengers on board, some of whom I was already acquainted with: Anderson and Delamaine, recently posted, like myself; the former to the 38th, and the latter to the 56th; also Miss Anson, who had come in the *Queen* and was on her way to join her father, Major Anson, at Indore.

My story will not be complete if I do not tell an incident of the trip: I suppose that the romance with which it was tinged impressed it on my memory. Of the friends I made on board, were two, St. John, a cadet like myself, and a Miss Elsham, and we became great chums. Miss Elsham was about seventeen, very pretty, with dark brown hair, and was what would now be called "a little fast," but the word was not coined then.

In the afternoons when the steamer stopped at the wood stations we three would go for walks, exploring, or else we would get one of the steamer's boats and go for a row. We had a great time! But after a while we found this walking and rowing made us all very hungry, the meals on board being over by the time we got back. What was to be done? Miss Elsham, in acknowledging to being "very hungry," said she was "very thirsty" also, and added that she liked beer, and liked it in a large glass! So one morning I interviewed the old khansamah (butler) to see how it could be managed. He agreed at last to have some supper for us, two grilled moorghees (chickens) and fried potato chips, not forgetting the beer! Miss Elsham's share, with a tall glass of beer, St. John and I took down to her cabin door by turns. Of course all this occasioned remarks. But there was one old lady on board who, we could see, was very wroth; still she said nothing, till one morning when I happened to go on deck a little earlier than usual and found Mrs. R—— there alone. Of course I had to say "Good morning," and then she attacked me; said we were making the girl as conceited as possible besides making a fool of her! (Here I thought her wrong; it seemed to me the other way about.) And then she added: "You know you can never marry her!" Now the idea of my joining my regiment for the first time with a wife so frightened me that I said: "I never thought of marriage!" "Then you ought to be ashamed of yourself!" she exclaimed. "Go away!" I bolted down below and told St. John, which so scared him that he did not appear on deck the whole day; the result being that the field was left clear for myself, and I enjoyed the society of Miss Elsham alone for that day.

The evening before we arrived at Allahabad, St. John and I had an unpleasant experience. For some days past Miss Elsham had been saying how she looked forward to finding some English letters awaiting her, and this put it into our heads to walk to Allahabad, after the steamer stopped, and get them for her. A more idiotic idea there could not be. In the first place, it was ten miles off; we should have to get a boat to cross the river when opposite the fort; there was no road, nothing but jungle through which we should have to make our way; and by the time we arrived the post office would be closed. However, we started, and that is about all we did do; for in about half an hour such a storm came on as took all the "gee" out of us. The rain came down in torrents, and we were drenched in no time; there was nothing for it but to go back. By this time it had become quite dark, and it was a mystery to me how we did not manage to walk into the river; as it was, we stumbled through every muddy pool in our way, and by the time we reached the steamer we were nice objects. We were "in white" when we started, and we were most certainly "in black" when we returned!

All the passengers were on deck watching the storm, and when Miss Elsham caught sight of us, miserable-looking objects as we were, I thought she would have had a fit! Wherever we stopped we left a muddy pool, and how they did laugh! I suppose she could not help it, but we thought it horrid of Miss Elsham. When I got below and began to change my things, I found I had lost my pocket-book containing a fifty-rupee note—all the money I had—and there were those suppers to be paid for!

St. John was very good about it, said he would go early with me in the morning and have a look for it. We got up at 4 A.M. and went; and under a tree, where we had tried to get shelter from the rain, found my book!

Next morning we arrived at Allahabad. I have never seen Miss Elsham since, and have often wondered what became of her. St. John was posted to the Bengal Fusiliers, became a famous Persian scholar, and was appointed secretary to the Board of Examiners at Fort William.

The next place I had to make for was Loodhianah, on the Sutlej; and now I was to have my first experience of travelling by dak, *i.e.*, in a palanquin borne by bearers. Anderson, who had been posted to the 38th N.I., went with me as far as Meerut. The journey, performed day and night, was somewhat monotonous, and I was not sorry when I reached Loodhianah, where I put up at the Dak Bungalow (Rest House). Up to this point I had travelled at Government expense, but now I had to depend on my own resources, and all the remaining distance had to be done by regular marches. How to do it I did not know. A horse or pony had to be bought, also saddle and bridle, tent, pots and pans, and tent furniture—and for all this I had not a rupee! Before leaving Calcutta it was impressed on me by the pay-master to be especially careful of a document he gave me, called "A Last Pay Certificate," as without it no pay would be forthcoming. Of course I had lost or mislaid this precious paper, and all applications for "pay" were in vain. While I was wondering what to do, a Major Creagh came and put up at the Bungalow on his way to Calcutta, *en route* to England. He came and asked me if I wanted a pony with saddle, etc., as he wanted to get rid of his—his dak (journey) being laid to Allahabad. I said Yes, I did want to buy one, but had no money. The following day he introduced me to a traveller who was going to Jullunder, as I was, and who, on hearing of my difficulty, most kindly offered to help me. In the first place he asked me to share his tent and be his companion on the road;

he had every requisite for the march, and he would be only too glad if I would go with him. He also offered to lend me a hundred rupees. Sydney Smith was his name, and I shall never forget his kindness. The consequence was, I got my pony, and we started two days after. How proud I was of that pony! my first possession in "horse-flesh". He was a good little beast, and I had him for many years; but he gave me several falls before I got accustomed to him. Smith was a good horseman and gave me several hints, so that after a little I did not do so badly. He rode a grey country-bred, good for work but a vicious brute. He had a trick of making a snap at you when you went near him, and this cost him dearly one day. We were encamped on the banks of the Ravee, and Smith told his syce (groom) to take the horse to the river and give him a bath and wash him well with soap. When the syce got him in the water and began to wash him, the brute made a grab at his hand, in which he was holding a piece of soap; instead of biting the man, he got hold of the soap which he bit savagely, and got it firmly fixed between his teeth. The syce threw water in his mouth and tried to get it out, but he only caused a lather which nearly drove the horse mad. The more he moved his jaws the worse it became, and it was two days before it all came away.

We had a delightful trip. Smith was most entertaining; he had travelled over Turkey and the greater part of Europe, and told many a story of his wanderings. He was excessively kind, and what I should have done had he not turned up, I don't know.

On arrival at Jullunder I reported myself to the brigade major (Major Palmer, 48th N.I.), and was told by him that I could not proceed farther, as the Killadar (Governor) of Fort Kote Kangra was holding the road against all comers; that a force was being got in readiness under Sir Hugh Wheeler to bring him to his senses; that I should be attached for the time being to one of the regiments, and when the affair was over could then go on to Noorpore.

This idea of seeing some service before joining my own regiment was grand, and Smith said he would come too and see the fun. Next day I found myself in orders to do duty with the 2nd Grenadiers, commanded by Colonel Hamilton. This gave me an opportunity of returning in a slight degree Smith's hospitality, as having a mess I could take him there as a guest; and this was not all, for that important document the "Last Pay Certificate" turned up! I could get some pay and refund him what he had lent me.

The march to Kote Kangra was uneventful but most enjoyable: climate and scenery all that could be desired. Our arrival there was followed by a demand to "Surrender"! And, on the killadar's refusal, preparations were made for an attack.

As soon as fire was opened from the siege train he changed his mind, and in two days the place was ours.

I went over the fort the next day. It was a dilapidated place, utterly incapable of standing against artillery, but most picturesquely situated on the summit of a hill. A river flowed round three sides at the base of precipitous rocks, a narrow road on the fourth side led to the gateway, and inside this a steep flight of stone steps led to the top, the view from which was very fine.

I had still some marches before me ere I eventually reached my destination; and as far as I could see they would have to be done alone, as Smith could go no farther; but Boswell, the adjutant, 2nd Grenadiers, told me that Major Abbott, Bengal Artillery, had been appointed commissioner of some of the newly acquired territory; that his work would take him past Noorpore, and that perhaps if I called on him he would let me join his camp. He, too, was most kind and gave me a cordial invitation. Hearing I had no tent, he said he would place one of his own at my disposal, and would be glad to see me as guest at his table.

He asked if I had a horse, and on my saying I had a pony, he remarked: "I should like you to ride one of mine while you are with me. You see, I am going to take charge of a large district, and we must make as good an appearance as possible. You shall have one of my Arabs and four sowars of my escort will be told off to attend you." Fancy! All this for a "griff" not yet joined! It was with sincere regret that I said good-bye to Smith, for he had indeed been helpful in every way. His last act was to make over to me one of his servants, a bearer, a capital fellow who remained in my service eleven years.

On joining Major Abbott's camp, I found, besides myself, Dan Robinson and Ralph Young, of the Engineers, who were to carry out the survey. The latter I knew well, as we were at Addiscombe together; so again my star was in the ascendant!

At this distance of time, I cannot recollect the number of marches there were between Kangra and Noorpore. I think twelve; but nothing particular occurred till we reached Fort Kotla. Here I quite unintentionally took a rise out of one of our senior captains that I don't think he ever forgot. It must be understood I did not know myself all that I had done until I joined my regiment.

Our camp was pitched in a lovely grove of mango trees; in front ran a small stream, and about a quarter of a mile beyond this rose a thickly wooded hill, on the summit of which was Fort Kotla. I can see it all now (1906) as plainly as I saw it then, and have rarely come across any scene more picturesque or beautiful.

Major Abbott told me that a detachment of my regiment (two companies), under a captain and two subalterns, were quartered in the fort, and that I ought to go and report myself. Accordingly I got my escort, without which I was never to go out, mounted and set forth. I may mention here that I found the Arab much easier to ride and manage than that little demon of a pony: the horse was a gentleman all over, while the pony was not. On reaching the foot of the hill I had to dismount and ascend a flight of stone steps, similar to those at Kangra. At the top I sent in my card and introduced myself to Captain Apthorp (commanding); Bennet and Priestly were his two subs., the former having been at Addiscombe with me. There was something in Captain Apthorp's manner I could not understand at all; it quite chilled one; and it was not till afterwards that I heard the reason.

It appears that when I left the camp with my sowars Apthorp was sitting at one of the windows in his shirt-sleeves, smoking, and saw me coming towards the fort, evidently to make a call. In his opinion no one had any right to go about with cavalry after him unless he had some position; so he hurried off to put on his uniform, telling his subs. to do the same; then all were ready to give the great man a proper reception when my card was put into his hand! The "great man" was only a "something sub. after all, and I have put on my jacket for him!" They told me that after I left his language was awful; nothing would pacify him. "Twenty-one years in the service to be made a fool of by a something sub.! What business has he to go about the country with a cavalry escort, as if he were commander-in-chief?"

Those of his own standing chaffed him about it a good deal, but we subs. never ventured to allude to the incident again. When I came to know him I liked him, and we were always good friends. He was a fine horseman, had the reputation of being about the best rider in India, possessed good horses, and was never better pleased than to get some of us together and take us across country; he was then in his element and was as cheery as possible.

Three marches from Kotla we arrived at Noorpore, where I parted from Major Abbott. A kinder-hearted man I never met, and afterwards, reading an account of the way in which he managed his district, I was not surprised to hear how beloved he was by all the inhabitants. Abbottabad, in the Punjab, will keep his name alive for all time.

With great regret I had to take leave also of my gallant Arab that had carried me so well. I had greatly improved in riding, and gained more confidence; my pony was a great come down!

Riding through the Bazaar I reached the gate of the fort and reported myself to the adjutant, and there was great joy when it was known I had arrived—not, be it understood, because such an important personage had joined, but because—I was the bearer of a large box of cheroots! This the postmaster at Jullunder had asked me to take charge of, as the mail carriers could not get past Kote Kangra.

For days past there had been nothing to smoke, so that my arrival was most welcome.

The whole regiment was quartered in the fort, which was much larger than either Kotla or Kangra, but, like these, built on a hill with steep, precipitous rocks on three sides; it also had a larger space outside the walls. The mess was in a large hall of one of the principal buildings, and high up, round three sides, ran a gallery, from which a number of small rooms branched off; one of these was allotted to me. It did not take long to settle down, as a bed, table, and chair constituted all our furniture.

CHAPTER II.

A FEW ANECDOTES.

First step—Slow promotion—Unmerited kudos—Monkey stories—Pity for the pony and its result—Doonga Singh, his capture and captivity—My first tiger hunt—A horse fair—Regiment marches to Delhi—I and the guide distinguish ourselves—A dog scare and a mishap.

THE next day I called on the commanding officer, Major Sibbald, destined to become one of the victims of the Mutiny. He was shot while commanding the Rohilcund Division. My regiment had been in the Sutlej Campaign, and was present at the battle of Sobraon, the 10th of February previous; several of the officers had been wounded, but only one, Lieutenant Scatcherd, killed. This gave me a step, making me fourth instead of fifth ensign.

Promotion had been terribly slow. Apthorp, when I had met him at Kotla, had only just been promoted after twenty-one years' service, and Brevet-Captain Saunders, adjutant at the time I joined, had been fifteen years an ensign!

After a few days Priestly was relieved at Kotla and joined the head-quarters, and from this time until I went home we became chums, and shared a house together for nine years. His father commanded the Irish Constabulary, and, previous to that, the 25th K.O.B.'s. Two of his brothers were at this time in the same regiment.

Our life at Noorpore was a very easy one: hardly any parades, as the ground did not admit of it; shooting and riding our chief pastime. On one occasion, by a mere fluke, I gained a great reputation as a shot. Priestly and I were on the parapet one day, and looking down we saw a large kite far away below us, whirling round in circles. I had a smooth bore in my hand at the time, loaded with ball, and without for a moment imagining that I could hit it, took aim, and knocked it over. I was never more astonished, but tried not to look it!

The place abounded with monkeys, and it was great fun to watch them when the men were cooking their dinners. As the chupatties were made they were placed on the ground in a pile; but the monkey would watch till the man's hands were occupied with kneading the dough, when he would pounce down, snatch one up and be off into a tree. The men being Hindoos put up with it very quietly. There was an old grey-bearded monkey that irritated Phibbs, one of our captains, immensely. In the afternoon when Phibbs wanted a quiet snooze, the beast would get on the roof over his head and jump about, drumming with his feet. One afternoon, Phibbs was in a tearing rage at this going-on, and taking up a golail (a pellet bow) said: "I'll stop him". Up he went by a narrow staircase that led to the roof, and getting to the top saw the monkey just opposite to him; he took careful aim, let drive, and hit the monkey on the nose. What happened then I, who was below, could only judge by the row and the awful language Phibbs was using, but he told me afterwards that the brute charged him like a battering ram, and that he lost his footing and fell down some of the stairs.

Noorpore could not be called a gay place, and I suppose it was the want of something to do that caused us sometimes to do stupid things. We got laughed at consumedly for the following:—

One evening after dinner, Priestly, Aikman, Gibbs and myself went for a stroll outside the fort. On a piece of ground, covered with scanty grass, a very miserable-looking pony was trying to get a feed. The air was keen and there was no blanket on him. One said, "What a shame to leave the poor pony out in the cold"; and after various expressions of pity, another said, "Let's drive him inside the fort!" But he would not be driven in, and went round in a circle; so, as he did not seem to know what was good for him, we determined to carry him in. We each took a leg, and off we staggered—he was far too much astonished to kick, so, I suppose, waited quietly to see the upshot. Presently we came to the road, and here was a slight dip, and down went the two carrying the fore legs with a crash. The sentry at the gate hearing the row, challenged. "Hookum dar?"

"Friend!" we shouted, and off we set again, up the steps, through the gate, and into the fort—the pony still quiet. The question was, where to put him? There were no stables. Unanimously it was resolved to take him to the mess, and in the mess he was put, but I must say the beast did not seem to appreciate all this kindness; outside, certainly, he got something to eat, though it was scanty, while here he got nothing. We turned in, quite satisfied with what we had done. Next morning there was a bit of a rumpus. The owner went early to fetch his quadruped, and, not finding him where he had left him, began to search and make inquiries. By chance he asked the sentry of the night before if he had seen his pony. "Yes," he said, "some of the 'Sahib Logue' (gentlemen) have got him. They carried him inside last night." When the owner got his pony he was not satisfied, because he said he had had no grass all night, as if *he* had turned him into a green pasture! It was a long time before we heard the last of this. Aikman died six months after, Gibbs at Mooltan in 1851, and poor Priestly in 1868.

In September orders came "to be in readiness to march to Nusseerabad in Rajpootana". We left in October. Priestly and I sharing a tent, as we had one each we were able to send one on ahead the night before, and have it ready pitched when we arrived. After going half a dozen marches we were joined by Lieut. Watson, Bengal Artillery, with two guns, for it was thought that the newly conquered Sikhs were inclined to give further trouble.

The fort at Jusmeerghur was in a very dilapidated condition, though formerly it must have been a strong place, unless artillery was brought against it. What remained of the walls was massive brick-work and was intact; these walls must have been fifty feet in height. A broad ditch surrounded the place.

Major Sibbald here left us for another regiment, and Major Halford from the staff joined us and took command.

During one of our riding expeditions, Apthorp came to great grief. We came to some very inviting hedges for jumping, and he and Bennet went at one together, but too close, for Bennet's horse swerved and caught Apthorp's horse on the quarter just as he rose to the jump. They both came a cropper, and Apthorp had three ribs broken.

We were about a month at Jusmeerghur, and then continued our march to Nusseerabad which we did not reach till the middle of January. Dates I am unable to give; all my memoranda and sketches of these times were lost in the Mutiny at Seetapore, and what I write is from memory alone.

Nusseerabad we liked much. The 37th N.I., Boileau's Camel Battery and Tait's Horse (3rd Irregular Cavalry) were also quartered there. After being alone so long the change was a most welcome one.

Twelve miles from us was Ajmere, a delightful place to go to for a change. A large bungalow, the property of Colonel Sutherland, governor-general's agent in Rajputana, was placed at our disposal whenever we chose to go. On two occasions when we made these trips Major Boileau sent his camel carriage for us, a most comfortable conveyance drawn by four camels, each camel being ridden by one of his men. As the road was sandy a greater part of the way they travelled over the ground well. The lake gave one boating and fishing, and there was shooting all round.

On one occasion, while I was there on leave, a raid was made on the treasury in Nusseerabad by a noted Rajpoot named Doonga Sing. The cause of it all, I believe, was that for some time past he had been petitioning Government regarding a grievance, and not getting, as he said, justice, or even being listened to, determined to have revenge.

He got together some horsemen and completely surrounded the paymaster's bungalow, which was separate from all the others by some little distance. Then going in himself with a few followers he cut to pieces a havildar's guard (sergeant) of my regiment that was there, not one escaping. He then took the treasure, about £30,000, loaded it on swift riding camels that he had waiting, and was off before any one knew anything about it.

When it was known in the lines, of course the cavalry were sent in pursuit; but it was too late:

they got clear away. It was all well planned and well carried out. Doonga Sing eluded capture for some time, but was caught at last, through the treachery, I believe, of one of his followers. He was brought to Ajmere and lodged in the jail, and a company of ours, under a captain and subaltern, was sent to keep guard. Brett's company, with myself as subaltern, had the first turn. The cells, in one of which Doonga Sing was confined, were three in number, forming one side of a court-yard surrounded by a high wall; iron gates composed of thick iron bars closed the cells, but afforded a free view of the prisoner. At night my bed was placed across the gate of his cell, and there I had to sleep.

Doonga Sing was a handsome old man; a long, white beard flowed down to his chest, and he had a very commanding and most dignified appearance. Hicks of the 37th asked leave to make a sketch of him. "No," he said, "not like this, with chains on. Doonga Sing should be drawn with a sword in one hand and a spear in the other, and *then* you might say, 'This is Doonga Sing!'" I talked with him sometimes, and rather admired him myself, in spite of what he had done, for no doubt he thought he had great provocation. He was tried at Ajmere and hanged in the jail. But before that took place my company was relieved, I am glad to say.

With regard to this episode of Doonga Sing, Captain Parrott of the 37th wrote some very amusing verses, the whole of which I cannot recollect, but one part ran :—

> Then raise your voices, let us sing
> Confusion to this robber king,
> Who made all Rajpootana ring
> By looting the Buckshee Khana.
> Some officers ran as hard as they could
> Intending to do no end of good,
> But devil a one was there who could
> Order the cavalry out, Sirs !

While we were at Nusseerabad, Priestly and I had our first experience of tiger shooting ; and taking into consideration how we went about it, I wonder I'm alive to tell the tale.

One day a native came in and told Priestly that a large tiger was lying down on the ground on the opposite side of a small stream that ran at the bottom of the parade ground. As there was no jungle there, only a few scattered bushes, Priestly would not at first believe him, but the man persisted that he was there ; so Priestly came to me, and we agreed to go in pursuit, and in order that they might enjoy the sport we decided to let our small "bow-wows" go with us. Hear it, O Shikaries! Two "griffs" armed with smooth bores, muzzle-loaded at that, with some small dogs setting forth to shoot a tiger !

On our way we picked up one or two more, anxious to be in at the death. (Whose ?)

There was no doubt in our minds that we should kill the tiger if he were there. All our talk was what we should do with the claws, the teeth, and the skin. Poor tiger, I wonder if he had any inkling as to what was coming! Before we reached the parade ground we met Major Biddulph of the 3rd Cavalry, who wanted to know what we were up to. We said we were going to shoot a tiger and then told him what the native said. He would not either at first believe that a tiger could be there, but, at last, after listening to the native's report, he said: "If the tiger is there and you attack him by yourselves, mark my words, there will be no shooting *him*, but *he* will make a meal off you and your dogs too. Wait till I get my rifle and I'll come with you to see fair play."

Now, we should have liked to do it all ourselves; but, as Biddulph was an old shikary, and one who had shot big game of all kinds, we were all very glad to have him with us, besides as he said to see "fair play". We none of us wished to take an unfair advantage of the tiger! When Biddulph joined us, off we set again and soon arrived at the small stream which was crossed by a small bridge. Here the native stopped and declined to go any farther; then pointing to a small maddar bush, about a hundred yards distant, said: "If the tiger has not moved, that is where you will find him". By this time our poor dogs were in a very dejected condition—I suppose they scented the beast; no more joyous barks and capers. They came along close to our heels, their tails between their legs.

Biddulph marshalled us in skirmishing order, himself in the centre, and begged us to be cool and not fire recklessly. If the tiger came out, those on his right were to fire first, so that all would not be unloaded at the same time; for there were no breech loaders then. When we got to within about forty yards of the bush, we saw him, that is, his head only as he looked up. Did we remember all we had been told? Not a bit of it! We fired a volley "ek sat" that would have done credit to any regiment in the service, and some one hit him on the jaw. That roused him with a vengeance, and he lightly jumped over the bush and came and laid himself down in the open, preparatory to a charge, showing his teeth and growling, his tail waving to and fro. Biddulph, who had reserved his fire, now let drive and wounded him mortally, but not sufficient to stop his charge. Down he came, direct at Biddulph, who, not having another barrel, knelt down and raised his rifle, holding it in front of him, horizontally, with both hands, and rammed it into the tiger's jaws; they both rolled over together, and when he got up the tiger was dead. If Biddulph had not come with us the result would have been, I am sure, very different. I never went out tiger shooting on foot again!

Pokur is a place about twelve miles beyond Ajmere. It is a very sacred place on the banks of a lake, where an annual horse fair was held. It is a very lovely spot. In the centre of the lake is an island, on which is a small temple of great sanctity, and to swim across to this and do poojah (prayers) is considered a most meritorious act. Pilgrims collect there in numbers, and in spite of the danger from the alligators essay the feat, many losing their lives in consequence. All of us that could get away made a point of attending, and for about ten days it was a most enjoyable picnic. Our camp was pitched in one of the groves of trees close to the water, and our amusements during the day were to visit all the camps of the horse merchants and try their cattle; also to watch the pilgrims. Some very good horses and ponies could be picked up at a reasonable price; they came chiefly from Cabul carrying apples. There were also some very good country-breds, especially from Kattiawar. These, curiously enough, were nearly all the same colour, namely, dun, black points, and a black mark running down the centre of the back. You could not have a better horse for work than one of these.

Parrott, of the 37th, who was a capital judge of a horse, generally accompanied us, and was a great help in giving his opinion.

In October, 1848, we marched to Delhi. How we grumbled at the hour of starting every morning! Our commanding officer was so afraid of the sun that the first bugle would sound at 3 A.M., and we would be off the ground by 4 A.M. It happened on one occasion that we arrived before sunrise. It was the custom every evening for the head-man of the village to supply three villagers to act as guides for the next day's march—one for the regiment, one for the advance-guard and one for the rear-guard. Sometimes these men knew the road and sometimes they did not, and on one occasion I got into a scrape through one not knowing the road. I had the advance-guard, and started about twenty minutes ahead of the regiment. It was pitch dark, and, although I had never been by this road before, I had my doubts. And sure enough when it was daylight, instead of being first in camp and ready to salute the regiment as it formed up, I found myself behind the rear-guard!

On going to the commanding officer I took care to push the wretched guide to the front to take all the blame. I must say, though, that I pitied him. The guides were brought overnight to the camp, as I said, and for security placed in the quarter-guard; they then had to walk the march, sometimes fifteen miles, receive the large sum of four annas (sixpence) and then trudge back again. No! I would not do it for the money.

Our commanding officer was about the worst rider that ever got on a horse; he never went out of a slow jog-trot, and was terribly nervous if any one rode up along-side of him. On one occasion, Priestly caught a pariah dog, tied an empty tin can to his tail, and then let him go. I was riding half-way up the column when this brute of a dog came tearing by me; my pony reared up straight on end and I went over his tail, and both pony and dog raced up to the head of the regiment where the commanding officer was riding. His rage was great, and but for his syce he would have been capsized also. When we arrived at camp he asked whose pony it was, and hearing it was mine, and that I had been thrown, rather hopefully asked if I had been hurt.

CHAPTER III.

DELHI—MOOLTAN—SEETAPORE.

Quartered at Delhi—A few incidents—Sir Charles Napier presents new colours—Society at Delhi—A joke at our expense—Ordered to Mooltan—March across the desert *via* Bikaneer—Arrival—Orders to build houses—Our difficulties, pecuniary and otherwise—An evening party—Annexation of Oudh—Step not popular with the sepoys—Ordered to Lucknow—Rumours of discontent—Proceed to Seetapore—Again ordered to build—Further disaffection—Outbreak at Meerut, 10th May, 1857—Our men declare their loyalty—Suspense—A period of waiting—Commissioner's offer refused—He holds back important letters from Sir H. Lawrence.

WE did not like Delhi so well as Nusseerabad. The 42nd N. I., the 50th N. I., and a battery of artillery were quartered there. The residents were very sociable and gave us a cordial welcome. Many of the friends I made there suffered in the Mutiny. After arrival the thing was to start on the rounds, as new-comers call first. At one of the places where I called I was so abashed that I had hardly a word to say. It was on the civil surgeon, and, when I went in, there were his wife and three daughters, and they all wore spectacles, and all four flashed them up at me together. The youngest of these, poor Maggie, who was a great favourite with every one, was barbarously murdered during the Mutiny at Hansi.

One day, when Priestly and I were calling here, we found to our annoyance that the commanding officer was making a call too, so we did not remain long; but on coming out there was a terrible rumpus. Our syces had allowed our horses to get too close together and they began to fight, the consequence being that Priestly's, in delivering a vicious kick at mine, missed him, but kicked the footboard clean off the commanding officer's buggy. Priestly jumped on his horse and bolted, and as I was getting on mine the commanding officer came out. Hearing what had happened he turned round upon me, thinking that my horse had done it. The syce exclaimed: "No, sahib, the other sahib's horse did it!"

Delhi and its vicinity were full of objects of interest, especially the Moti Musjid, the ruins of the old city and the Kootub, fifteen miles from cantonments. One, which was often at that time passed by us without notice, was to become in after years worthy of as much as any of the first-named places, *viz.*, the famous Ridge that extended from the Cashmere Gate of the city to cantonments.

While we were there, Sir Charles Napier, commander-in-chief, arrived, and for three days previous a guard of honour, consisting of a battalion, encamped within the city walls in readiness to receive him. The brigadier sent down his tents and treated us royally, all being his guests for the time being.

On this occasion the chief presented us with new colours, the old ones being placed in the church.

One of the duties was "main guard" over the Cashmere Gate relieved weekly, a subaltern commanding, who during that time had to keep within the city walls, and in fact always well within call; for, if the old king passed and there was no one to salute him, it would have been *unpleasant!*

There were several English residing in the city, and all were most hospitable. Two ladies, Mrs. Foster and Mrs. Fuller, the former of whom had two daughters, were always glad to see one. All, save one of the daughters, were murdered by the mutineers.

An absurd thing happened at one of their parties. Priestly and I received an invitation to a dance, and at the bottom of the card was put "camp fashion". This meant that each guest had to bring his own knives, plates and glasses—a very usual thing. Now, neither Priestly nor I had any champagne glasses, so we told our servants that before they went to the house they were to buy two long glasses (lumber pyalas), not the common kind, but good ones—handsome cut glasses. Well, we had our dance, and on going into the supper-room heard shrieks of laughter from those who were before us! What did we see when we went in? Our khitmatgars (servants) had put our plates alongside of each other, knives, wine-glasses all correct, but each plate flanked by two enormous glass flower-vases about a foot and a half high, big enough to hold a bottle of champagne in each. This was a native's idea of handsome champagne glasses! There both the culprits stood behind our chairs looking at the effect with the greatest complacency. We did not hear the last of it for some time.

Before we left Delhi one of the Miss Fosters was married to Stevens, our adjutant, and the other to Lieutenant Burgess, 74th Regiment.

We were only at Delhi a year; in 1849 we were ordered to Mooltan. On the route arriving, we found we were to march *viâ* Bikaneer, and from thence crossing a sandy desert to Bhawulpore, and then on to our station. It was an experiment. No regiment had ever marched that way before, and a report was to be sent in of our experience. At Bikaneer the desert commenced, and the commanding officer decided to cross by wings; and, in order that we should not miss the direction, fires were lighted at intervals. It being the cold weather, there was no earthly reason why we should not have waited till day-break before starting. But no, he would go in the dark. It was the heaviest tramp I ever had, sinking into the sand well above the ankles; but I was fascinated by the strange, weird scene—as far as one could see nothing but sand, and this in huge hillocks. Imagine the sea in a heavy gale of wind suddenly congealed. This gives an exact idea of it. I never heard what the commanding officer said in his report; not much in favour of the route, I fancy, for we were the first and last that ever marched that way.

We arrived at Mooltan on Christmas Eve, 1849, and took up our quarters in the fort, which had only recently been captured after severe fighting. Of course we had to rough it a bit, but the rooms were not so bad, and, as a consolation, there was no house rent; but, after wasting all the cold weather, in March orders arrived to have a site for cantonments marked out on a piece of ground about two miles off, and to commence the lines forthwith. This meant that officers were to build their own houses. Pleasant news for the impecunious sub.! The ground that was marked out for Priestly and me, two separate plots, we joined into one, and forthwith built the stables, which we used as a dwelling while our house was being built. Long before we vacated the fort the weather set in very hot, and to ride down in the day-time to superintend the work in uniform—tight red jacket and forage cap—which the commanding officer insisted on our wearing, was not pleasant. The 12th N.I. and 5th Irregular Cavalry were there as well as ourselves.

The trouble we had with the workmen! Their utter indifference to a straight line and as to whether a wall was perpendicular or not! If we showed them it was not upright, the answer invariably was: "Never mind, sahib; it will be all right when we put on the plaster!" I wonder some of us were not buried in the ruins. As soon as a house was finished a house-warming was *de rigueur*, and then one had to stand the comments on the architecture, etc.; but it was great fun on the whole. Occasionally you would see a house partially built but deserted—no workmen. This meant that the owner had no more money, and had gone to look for some. When ready to go on again his state was indeed parlous, for he had to look for his workmen, many of whom he would find were gone to some one else. Priestly was architect of ours, and he built a very good one—a sitting-room, large hall, and a bedroom on each side—four rooms in all, a broad verandah running all round. It cost altogether about 4,000 rupees.

Once every year after the inspection the commanding officer used to give a dinner. He never invited any one not in the regiment, and as he never unbent—always had the parade manner on more or less—these parties were dreary in the extreme. I recollect on one occasion when certainly a little life was put into the meeting, but decidedly at my expense. When we went into the drawing-room after dinner, Mrs. Halford apologised for not being able to give us some music, as her piano had not arrived; and then suddenly, fixing her eye on me, she said: "But I know what will amuse you". She walked over to the bookcase and took down two large music books; these she brought to me, put them into my hands, and said: "Will you please whistle the Irish Quadrilles for us? The music is in these books." She then complacently resumed her seat. Can any one imagine a more awful situation than mine?—those two big books on my knee, all except the commanding officer laughing as if they would never stop. For, as they told me afterwards, they were immensely tickled with the idea that my whistling could afford them any amusement, even with the help of the music, of which I did not know a note.

In 1852-53 Colonel Halford was transferred to the 71st, and Major Birch got command of the regiment.

During this year, 1853, I returned home in order to be married to Miss Bateman, daughter of General Bateman, an old Peninsula veteran; and in 1854 I rejoined my regiment at Etawah, where the right wing was now stationed, the left wing being at Mynpoorrie. Here we remained till the end of '55, when, the annexation of Oudh having been determined upon, we were ordered to join a force collecting at Cawnpore, under orders to proceed to Lucknow. I do not think this step was at all popular with the sepoys (native soldiers). Oudh was the province where we got our best men, and the regiment was chiefly composed of men from that part; and then, all of them, more or less, being landowners, by aiding us in the annexation they considered they were giving us the land, and expected something in return. It is true that bribery, corruption and misgovernment prevailed to a terrible extent, but all this did not affect the sepoy and his family in the same way as it did the rest of the peasantry, and I will explain why.

Cases were of every-day occurrence in the civil courts of crops being stolen—cut during the night; land boundaries encroached upon, and such like. In the majority of these cases the injured would be a poor man, and it was almost hopeless for him to obtain justice. Money was required to have his petition drawn up, to pay a vakil, or lawyer; money was required to bribe the attendance of the court, to enable him to present it, and, supposing he managed all this and brought his witnesses, he would be confronted by his opponent, in nine cases out of ten a rich man, who would have any amount of bought witnesses to swear what he pleased. But supposing this poor peasant had a son in the service, it was another thing entirely. Before enlisting he was made part-owner in his father's property, he would join his regiment, and some while after, perhaps, he would receive a letter from home to the effect that the crops were carried off. Two courses were open to him: first of all he represented the case to the commanding officer who would order the interpreter to draw up a statement which he might take himself if he could obtain leave, and present himself, and being known as a sepoy no one would dare to prevent him from going into court. If he could not get leave, the statement, accompanied by a power of attorney, would be sent by the commanding officer himself to the British resident at the court of Oudh, who would forward it to the magistrate of the district, and he in turn would send for the complainant and defendant, and the case would be decided on its merits, the whole expense to the sepoy being eight annas (one shilling) for the stamped paper. This was one reason why the Company's service was so popular.

A little incident that happened on the first march towards Lucknow will serve to show in what light they looked on the whole movement. Some sepoys went to a wood-seller and took some of his wood for cooking purposes. When the man asked for payment they refused, saying that everything in Oudh now belonged to the sirkar (Government), that they had given it all, and that they, being the sirkar's soldiers, could take what they liked. They were made to pay, and I know that they thought it very unjust.

There was no opposition to the annexation at Lucknow. The king was deposed and sent to Calcutta, and the force was broken up; regiments were told off for their several stations. Our destination was Seetapore, fifty miles north-west of Lucknow.

Here we had to build again, but in this case were helped by Sir James Outram, the then resident and commissioner, who gave us a Government grant—a subaltern got 600 rupees, the higher grades more in proportion. I believe Government gave him a snub for it.

Besides ourselves there was a squadron of 15th Irregular Cavalry and two regiments of Oudh Irregular Infantry.

In the beginning of the cold weather, 1856, we heard rumours of disaffection in the regiments down country, in the end leading to their disbandment; then that this feeling extended to stations higher up; until at last the news of the outbreak at Meerut on the 10th of May, 1857, and the subsequent massacre of Europeans at Delhi reached us. During all this time the men were just as well acquainted with all that was going on as we were, if not better; and thinking, I suppose, that they might be suspected, took every opportunity of assuring us of their loyalty; on one occasion saying that if the whole army went they would remain staunch.

Now I don't know if others experienced the same feelings, but to me this period of suspense was the most trying time of all. We could do nothing but wait, and wait for we knew not what. We believed in our men, but still the question would be asked: "What was there in them to make them different from the others, if all chose to go?" The commissioner of the district, who had a house in the civil lines outside military cantonments, sent a letter to the commanding officer stating that he was provisioning his bungalow in case of emergencies, and had directed all those under him to assemble there should an outbreak take place, and suggesting that all military officers should be ordered to do the same. The commanding officer submitted this proposal to us all, and I was glad to see the senior officers were against it; I was only junior then, but I opposed it all I could. It was utterly impracticable. Fancy trying to hold a bungalow, a one-storeyed dwelling with a thatched roof! This could be fired at once, and out you must come. It was given up as far as we were concerned, and instead we agreed to meet at the commanding officer's house and act as circumstances directed.

The commissioner, Mr. Christian, was very obstinate, and stuck to his own plan; he also, as we heard afterwards, kept back a letter that he had received from Sir Henry Lawrence. This letter requested him to send all the ladies and children into Lucknow, and quarters would be provided for them in the Residency. Without saying a word to any one, he took upon himself the responsibility of declining this offer, saying that he could provide for the safety of all under him. How terribly he and his suffered for this the end proved. As he and Mrs. Christian ran out they were immediately shot down. Their little girl, Sophie Christian, was saved by her ayah, who concealed her; and she eventually came safe home to England.

An important law case arose out of the deaths here related. When at home a solicitor came to call on me to ascertain, if possible, which of the two, the commissioner or his wife, died first. I told him it was impossible for me or any one else to say, and that the best course would be to divide what money depended on the results of the answer to this question. I believe this was done.

In addition to Mr. and Mrs. Christian, Mr. and Mrs. Henry Thornhill and their children, and several others also lost their lives. Those escaping divided into two parties as follows: (1) Lieutenant Burnes, Sir Mountstuart and Miss Madeline Jackson, Sergeant-Major Morton, and little Sophie Christian. These found refuge, although reluctantly, with Rajah Lonee Singh, at his fort of Mithowlee. (2) Mrs. Greene, Miss Jackson and Captain John Hearsey fled northwards, and after being joined by other refugees found shelter at Mutheearee with the Rajah of Dhoreyrah. The first-named party, after most terrible sufferings, were all murdered with the exception of Madeline Jackson. Miss Jackson and her sister were both extremely pretty girls, and only a few days before the outbreak had spent the day at our house.

CHAPTER IV.

OUTBREAK OF MUTINY.

Outbreak at Seetapore—The parade of the regiment—Officers killed and wounded—Friendly sepoys—Flight into Lucknow—Incidents attending it—Privation—Terrible heat—Help from Lucknow—We reach the garrison—All's well.

AT last our turn came! On the 1st of June at 11 A.M., a subadar (native officer) went to the commanding officer's house and reported that he had very good grounds for believing that the men of the other two regiments intended to make a dash for the treasury and loot it; that he had ordered the regiment to fall in quietly, and now asked the commanding officer to come and take command with the object of protecting the sirkar's property.

The major got his horse and all went down to the parade where the men were drawn up in line; after a few words with the native officers he rode to the front and gave the word, "Fours right". And then directly after he gave the order, "Quick march". A sepoy then ran up and shot him in the back, and he fell from his horse dead. Lieutenant Smalley was immediately killed by a bayonet thrust, as also the sergeant-major. Graves, the adjutant, was wounded in the head, and a havildar (sergeant), who called out, "Don't kill the Sahib Logue," was immediately bayoneted.

Some of the men were passive in the matter, and these pushed us clear of the others, saying: "We can do nothing for you. Leave this and get away as fast as you can." We hurried back to the commanding officer's, and found all assembled as had previously been arranged. It was a sad task, telling Miss Birch the news of her father's death.

The thing now was to get away to Lucknow, and that as fast as possible, while the men were busy looting the treasury. We had just time to get some of our horses out. It was not pleasant having to abandon everything — clothes, books, pictures, sketches and furniture; but it had to be done, so regrets were useless. During the time of waiting, inquiry was made if all were present, when a German bandmaster we had behaved in a most cowardly way. As the pay was good and a house found him, he brought out his father from England, a very old man, feeble and incapable of making any attempt to move himself, and there was delay in providing him with a vehicle. His son was in such dread of the sepoys that, fearing they would come before we could get away, he exclaimed: "Oh, leave him behind!" I am thankful to say the poor old man reached Lucknow in safety.

We started, in all about sixty, thirty being friendly sepoys of my regiment, the 41st N.I. These men must at this period have been friendly disposed, and yet within a fortnight of entering Lucknow they could not any longer be trusted—a mysterious thing, and one that was never accounted for. These men were therefore given the option of returning to their homes, which they gladly agreed to without exception, not one remaining with us officers whose lives they had helped to save. This fact shows that there was some strong undercurrent of disaffection running through them. Possibly they were in communication with the rebels outside; or, again, the hardships they had to endure may have proved too great for them. On our arrival in Lucknow these sepoys were received by Sir Henry Lawrence, who highly praised their devotion, promised them rewards, and placed them under their own commander, Major Apthorp.

Now for the journey. I don't suppose it possible to make any one understand what the heat was. It was blowing half a gale, and the wind was as if it came from the hottest furnace. The road at first took a curve leading to a village, Khyrabad, a place we knew to be full of fanatical Mohammedans. This we thought it best to avoid, so took a line across country and came into the road beyond the village. Most fortunate was it for us that we did so, for we heard afterwards that having looted the treasury the sepoys came in pursuit of us, but, hearing at Khyrabad that we had not passed, concluded that we had gone some other way, and so returned. We should certainly have been murdered if they had caught us up. That bit across country was not easy with the vehicles we had ; a dogcart in which we had put a few things from the mess was upset twice, and others had continually to be helped out of some difficulty or another by literally "putting one's shoulder to the wheel". The wife of one of the bandsmen died from sunstroke, and in addition to all this there was the fear of our falling in with some of the disbanded regiments that were all over the country making their way towards Delhi. That night we rested in a grove of trees, half our number on guard. We procured a few chupatties and chutney from a village, and, more precious than all, some water melons, for we had had nothing to drink since we started, and our thirst was great. We managed to persuade a coolie to start off as quickly as possible to Lucknow with a note telling of our condition, as, for all we knew, the road might not be open, the troops forming the garrison at Lucknow having mutinied also.

We started again as soon as it was light and trudged on somewhat refreshed after a comparatively cool night, and at about 5 P.M. to our great joy saw Europeans coming to meet us. It was a party of volunteer cavalry, military and civilians, composed of some who, like ourselves, were refugees from the district. They brought with them carriages and refreshments, and, as we had been without food for nearly thirty hours, the latter were more than acceptable. Finally we reached the Residency all safe about 8 P.M., and it is impossible to describe the feeling of relief and security at hearing as we passed through the Bailey Guard an English sentry calling out: "All's well!"

CHAPTER V.

SIEGE OF LUCKNOW.

My prediction verified—Commissioner's house fired—Names of those who perished—Other losses at Seetapore—Mrs. Stuart saved—Just retribution—Report myself to Sir J. Inglis—Given charge of the church—Incidents while there—On sick list—News of Cawnpore massacre—Chinhut—Terrible fate of friends—Return to vestry—Church destroyed—Death of Sir H. Lawrence—Grief of the garrison—His foresight—Disaster to the cattle—Serious attack on Redan battery—Enemy's great daring—Lieutenant Grant's death—Mutineers send me a message—Rebels make their fiercest attack—Dangers to the garrison—Great heat causes many deaths—Prices of provisions—Great scarcity—End of July—Many casualties—Strange recovery of Lieutenant Charlton—A droll incident—A memorable night—Ungud goes out successfully—He returns—Several deaths—Small-pox and cholera raging in the garrison—Great food privations—Remarkable death of Ensign Studdy, 32nd Foot—Residency vacated—General attack—Followed by others.

I MAY state here what we heard, but not for some time after, of what occurred in the civil lines and other parts of Seetapore. Strange to say, what I said regarding the futility of holding a bungalow was verified. The Commissioner's house was surrounded, an arrow with a piece of lighted tow was fired into the thatch, which was immediately in a blaze, and as the Commissioner and his wife ran out they were shot down.

Captain Doran, commanding one of the Irregular regiments, managed to escape with his wife into the country, but they had not gone far before they were overtaken. Captain Doran had a double-barrelled gun in his hand. The rebels swore to preserve both his and his wife's life if he would give up the gun. He hesitated for a long time, and at last surrendered it. They instantly shot him with it, but let his wife go. She, poor woman, went back to their house and was concealed by her ayah, and by her help succeeded at last in reaching the Residency, disguised as a native woman, being obliged to hide for a fortnight in a village, but having been kindly treated *en route*. Mrs. Doran and Lieutenant Burnes were the only ones of the 10th Regiment who escaped with their lives from Seetapore. In the 9th Regiment, also at Seetapore, the only one who escaped with her life was Mrs. Greene, wife of Lieutenant Greene, every one else being murdered.

Mrs. Doran was killed during the siege. Sir Mountstuart Jackson of the Civil Service and his two sisters managed to get away, but were taken prisoners afterwards and conveyed to the city of Lucknow. One sister escaped, but the other, with her brother, was murdered. I had the satisfaction of being the means of saving one life. Captain Stuart, who was attached to us as interpreter, believing in the idea of holding the bungalow, had actually sent his wife there on the morning of the 1st, before the outbreak. I knew of this only about 9 A.M., but immediately went to him and begged him to fetch her away, I felt so certain it would never answer. It was a long time before I could persuade him, but at last he did so. Hardly were they within our lines again before the mutiny broke out and the Commissioner's bungalow was fired.

One thing that happened after we left I was delighted to hear; just retribution did fall at least on one miscreant. It was told me by our Bazaar chowdrie, who came to see me some years afterwards. The people round about Seetapore are of a low caste, called Pasees, and are armed with bows and arrows. Of course they did not dare to come across any of the sepoys, or try to get any loot, as their career would soon have been cut short; but they hovered about on the outskirts, looking for a chance. Now one of our sepoys, after getting his share of rupees, went to the colonel's house to see what there was he could take away. In the stable were a pair of horses, and a carriage in the coach-house. A bright idea seized him. He put the horses to, then went into the house and took whatsoever attracted his fancy, piled it all into the carriage, got up on the box and drove off in triumph, no doubt thinking what a swell he would be in his own village; but although he did not know it, his time was come. One of the Pasees saw what was going on, and watched him, and when he found out the road he intended taking, ran ahead across the fields and lay in ambush. As my friend in the carriage passed, to his surprise he got an arrow through his temple which tumbled him off the box, and he never rose again. I would have given that Pasee bakshish if I had met him.

The day after reaching the Residency, June 3rd, I went to report myself to Colonel (afterwards Sir John) Inglis, and, as help was needed in superintending the stowing away of grain that was coming in in quantities, he sent me to the church with orders to make it into a granary. It was not at all nice work, having to pull everything to pieces—the pews, pulpit, everything had to come away—but it had to be done, and when all was clear the whole space inside was filled with sacks of grain. Meanwhile I had taken up my quarters in the vestry.

A few days after this another officer was sent to help, a Captain Barlow, who had been major of brigade to the Oudh force. A more excitable man I never met; it seemed that he could not stand all that was happening; he was in the vestry with myself, but he had such disturbed nights I could hardly get any rest. At last the idea seized him that I wanted to murder him, and his yells were awful. Then I thought it time that a doctor should see him, and he was ordered to the hospital. There his cries at night for help and assistance still continued, and I was told that a private who was a patient there cursed me, because my name was continually dinned into his ears. Poor Captain Barlow! He did not live long, but retained his hallucination to the last.

A severe attack of ophthalmia blinding me for the time, rendered me perfectly helpless, and during the time I was laid up the disaster at Chinhut occurred, and we were then besieged in earnest. I must not forget to relate the adventures of an officer of ours, Lieutenant Inglis, who at the time of the outbreak was at Mullaon, a small place not far from Seetapore, in command of a detachment. When his men heard what had happened at head-quarters, as a matter of course they followed suit, and sent the native officer to him to request he would march them to Delhi. Inglis said, "No! But I'll march the men to Lucknow!" This the men would not have, and again the native officer came to him telling him this, and very coolly added that they were going to take the treasure. "Very good," returned Inglis, "I cannot prevent you; but as you are going to appropriate the money I beg to remind you my last month's pay is due, and that amount you must hand over to me." The native officer admitted that this was right, but when the matter was put to the sepoys they refused; and, finding he could do nothing, he got on his horse and made off, only just in time. He made for the palace of a rajah in the neighbourhood, who protected him, and eventually he succeeded in getting into Lucknow disguised as a native woman, carried in one of the small palanquins women go about in. He was afterwards severely wounded by the fragments of a shell, and the doctors said they never had a better patient: he never complained and took everything as quietly as possible.

I shall never forget the time when the news reached us, about the 28th of June, of the massacre at Cawnpore. I was lying in a room in the Residency, quite blind from the effects of ophthalmia, when a doctor came in whose wife had been left at Cawnpore under the idea she would be safer there than at Lucknow. Poor fellow, it was terrible to witness his grief. All night long he paced the room, except when at intervals he would throw himself on the floor and roll about in agony of mind. Amongst those who suffered on that occasion were two dear friends of mine, Dr. and Mrs. Harris; he had been surgeon of my regiment, 41st N.I., during the march from Delhi to Mooltan, but left us at the latter station to take up a civil appointment. Shortly before, in 1856, I had been staying with them at Jounpore, and I little thought when I said "good-bye" that such a terrible fate was in store for them. From the accounts given by natives afterwards of what took place, it appears that when the order was given to separate the men and women it was found impossible to part them. Mrs. Harris had her arms round her husband's neck, and nothing could make her loosen her hold. They were then both cut down together.

As soon as I was well enough I went back to the church and superintended the giving out of grain. Day by day the poor little church was getting smaller and smaller. Round shot had taken off all the ornamental finials on the roof, and there were great breaches in the walls; it only just lasted as long as the grain, and then I went to another granary.

One morning I was rather startled by what I saw on awakening: the body of a man had been brought into the churchyard and left there till some one had time to dig a grave. His attitude was as if in conflict with an opponent, his right arm being raised, the eyes wide open and fixed in a glassy stare straight at me; and, as he was but about four feet from me, the sight, under the circumstances and surroundings, gave me an ugly shock.

Up to the present date, July 2nd, Sir Henry Lawrence had been Commissioner and Commandant of the Lucknow garrison. Although in failing health, he had continued to perform his duties, but to many his health gave cause for great anxiety; the strain was evidently proving too much for a man of his age. He occupied a room in the Residency which was greatly exposed to the rebels' fire. Although frequently begged to vacate this, he refused, and only the day before this date a shell had burst in, but without doing injury to any one. About 9 A.M. on the 2nd of July an eight-inch shell entered the room by the window and burst, wounding Sir Henry in the hip, and slightly injuring Captain T. F. Wilson, D.A.A.G., who was standing by his bed. His nephew, Mr. G. H. Lawrence, C.S., who was in the room, escaped uninjured. He was taken to the house of Dr. Fayrer (now Sir Joseph Fayrer), where he lingered till the 4th. His emaciated condition and the nature of his wounds rendered any thought of an operation impossible; his sufferings in the meanwhile were most piteous. Those gathered by his bedside soon realised that the end was near, and to all the loss of such a man at such a crisis was truly irreparable. His personal gifts, as well as his great abilities, and added to these his lovable disposition, had endeared him to all, every one present being moved to tears; there was not a dry eye in the room. Truly a great man was passing away amidst agonising sufferings, whilst outside shots were continually striking the verandah on which he lay. During his intervals of freedom from pain, he exhorted all around him to be sparing of their ammunition, and at all costs to "save the ladies".

His death cast a great shadow over the garrison, and at such a time was most depressing to all concerned. His uprightness, unselfishness, and genial, affectionate nature made us all feel that we had indeed lost a friend, and that in a time of great need. Before dying Sir Henry appointed as his successors Major Banks to be Chief Commissioner, Colonel Inglis to command the troops of the garrison, and Major J. Anderson to command artillery and direct engineering operations.

It was entirely owing to Sir Henry's foresight that the garrison of Lucknow was enabled to hold out so long, both in provisions and in ammunition. Indeed, under Providence we were all indebted to this great hero for preservation from famine.

About the middle of July we had a disaster with the cattle that had been driven in for our use. The boosah (chopped straw) intended for their food was stacked in the racquet court, filling it level with the top of the walls. One night it rained, the boosah swelled, and down came the walls like a pack of cards! The boosah remained standing. Then D—— of my regiment was told off to look after the bullocks, and see that they did not get at it; but he was a very poor herdsman and allowed them to do as they liked; so they ate and ate till they undermined it, and then down it came, smothering five of them. Of course we had them for rations, but it was too much wholesale slaughter for a beleaguered garrison; so D—— was taken off duty. If he had only heard what was said of him, —well, he wouldn't have liked it.

On July 20th a very serious attack had been made. A mine was sprung near the Redan battery, evidently intended to destroy it, but fortunately this failed, the enemy missing the right direction. This was followed by an assault on our entire position; a terrible fusillade of round shot and musketry was directed upon us, the enemy advancing, under cover of this, quite close up to our defences. At the Redan they came within twenty-five paces of the battery, which was under the charge of Lieutenants

F. Cunliffe and MacFarlane; but they were met by a heavy fire and retired with great loss. Many of them gathered round the bastion, which we called Grant's, and to dislodge them Lieutenant Grant (Bombay Army), who had been stationed at Duriabad, was throwing a hand-grenade, but unfortunately held it a little too long and it burst in his hand, shattering it completely and wounding Captain H. Forbes, who commanded, at the same time. Grant's hand was amputated, but he died from the effects a few days after, having previously lost his wife and daughter from cholera. He left two little orphans, one quite a baby. The engagement lasted from early morning till 4 P.M. Happily, our losses were but four killed and twelve wounded, whilst the rebels lost some hundreds. This day's work gave us confidence, as we were convinced that we could hold our own against their greatest efforts.

Apthorp of ours had a post looking on to the Cawnpore Road, and one day he told me that some of the enemy for the last two or three nights had come up close underneath his walls, and called out that they would let the quartermaster from Seetapore come out and get clear away if he liked. As I was quartermaster of my regiment, this must have been meant for me. If I had accepted the offer, I wonder how far I should have got! All this time firing went on continually, day after day, without cessation; and when, as I suppose, they were hard up for shells, curious missiles were sent. One day when I was at the church I watched one in the air that had just been fired from a mortar. On it came, high up, then gradually descended and dropped into an open grave. It was a log of wood, partially hollowed out, and stuffed with combustibles; it did not do the least harm.

On July 21st (my birthday) the enemy, still undeterred, made their fiercest attacks which lasted throughout the day. They had discovered our weak side, and proceeded to undermine by digging a hole in the wall of an enclosure which skirted a compound on that side, a screen of canvas and a low wall alone separating them from us. The danger at this moment was great, and but for our concentrating our forces immediately at this spot the siege of Lucknow might have ended in a different manner.

While these operations were going on, Major Banks was struck in the temple by a bullet and killed instantaneously. He was incautiously looking out upon the enemy, poor fellow, and never moved again. A great stand was here made by us, and after two hours a mortar was brought down and opened upon the rebels. This caused the mutineers quickly to disperse, and as they fled a heavy fire was opened upon them from the brigade mess. Late in the afternoon the body of Major Banks was sewn up in a white sheet, this being now the only way available, since deaths had become so numerous that the making of coffins was impossible, often several bodies being buried in the same grave. Added to this, the heat was very great, and at times, in spite of precautions, the evil smells were most offensive, the odours arising from the dead and unburied cattle, and the offal of the slaughtered beasts, making it almost unbearable. Under these conditions it was not surprising that we had many deaths from disease at this time. Lieutenant Dashwood of the 48th N.I. and the Rev. Mr. Polehampton both died from cholera. Mr. Polehampton had just recovered from a severe wound, when he was taken ill and carried off in a few days. Colonel Halford, who formerly commanded my regiment, died on the 29th from a carbuncle, and Mrs. Thomas, wife of Lieutenant Thomas, Madras Artillery, and Mrs. Edgar Clarke, wife of Lieutenant Clarke, Assistant Commissioner of Gondalo, of small-pox on the 16th and 30th respectively.

Unquestionably the sufferings among the children were even greater than those of adults, and many parents were left childless at the close of the siege. It is never fit for European children to be in the plains during the hot season, but when privations and want of proper food were added to intense heat, it can be easily understood that the mortality was great among them; as many as fifty succumbed, I believe. Then again the pest of flies was most trying, and as we had no coolies to work the punkahs to abate this nuisance they swarmed in myriads. Lucknow had always been noted for this pest in the hot season. Dr. Brydon (the only survivor of the Cabul Massacre) was wounded while at dinner, the bullet completely traversing his body. Every day some one was hit.

Provisions had become very scarce: a ham that was put up for auction at this time fetched 100 rupees (£10), and a moorghee (chicken) fifty rupees (£5), half a bottle of honey forty-five rupees—one might never have to pay for it, so it did not much matter! Money was plentiful, and none of us were sure if we should ever be able to spend it.

By the end of July our casualties had greatly increased, and in the 32nd Regiment alone 170 losses had occurred from sickness and wounds; this regiment mostly consisted of Cornishmen. The following also were killed: Mr. Bryson, sergeant of the Volunteer Cavalry, shot dead on the 9th of July; Lieutenant Arthur, 7th Light Cavalry, and Lieutenant Lewin, Artillery, both shot dead at the Cawnpore Battery, which was in a very exposed position and in consequence cost us many brave lives.

Two of our European clerks and a son of the superintendent of the Civil Department were all killed about this time. In one instance Lieutenant Charlton of the 32nd received a wound in the back of his head from a bullet which penetrated to the brain; he was considered by the doctors a hopeless case, but nevertheless recovered, and lived to go home, to every one's great astonishment; nine months after the bullet appeared on the surface of the wound and was then extracted. Among the list of wounded were the following: Lieutenants Bryce, O'Brien, Harmer and Edmondstoune, Captain Boileau, Mr. G. H. Lawrence, C.S., Lieutenant D. C. Alexander, Captain Barlow, my companion in the vestry, and Mr. Heley, 7th Cavalry, who afterwards died.

Although there were these dire straits within the garrison, a very droll incident occurred among us about this time. A certain medical officer, thinking that he overheard a brother medico speaking slightingly of his behaviour, and attributing to him a want of courage, "went for him," and fisticuffs were followed by arrest, so here was double torture! Whilst held in durance vile by the rebels outside, he was also under arrest by his commanding officer inside to the end of the siege, only being allowed to visit his wife occasionally; of course at the end of the siege nothing more was heard of the incident.

The following night was a memorable one with us, as we were enabled to send a native messenger named Ungud with a despatch written by Mr. Gubbins to General Havelock, telling of our position, circumstances and details of our own forces and that of the enemy as far as was known to us. Ungud got away safely under cover of heavy rain and darkness, eluding the sentinels of the enemy. Readers will remember the name of Mrs. Doran, one of our Seetapore refugees, whose husband was killed before her eyes, being shot by the rebels with his own rifle, she escaping dressed as a native woman. Well, this poor lady was herself shot dead by a matchlock ball, after it had traversed two suites of rooms, reaching her in a standing position. Her death was greatly deplored, as she had been so helpful to all around her. A real heroine, this woman!

To our great joy, on the 25th Ungud returned with news of Havelock's force, and that we might hope to meet it in the course of five or six days. For some days past we had daily lost several precious lives; the natives had become despondent and desertions were more frequent among them; so nothing could have been more timely than this news, and we all felt vastly relieved. As Ungud was himself a native it gave them the greater confidence in his statements, which he freely furnished them with; they bombarded him with shoals of questions, all of which he gladly answered, and they were thus satisfied. Meanwhile Ungud brought us much other information. One thing that was very sad indeed was the terrible account of the Cawnpore massacre of the women and children, by that demon Nana, all of which turned out to be even less than the facts. He could also give us some details of the doings of the rebels, and from him we learnt that the Risaldar of Fisher's Horse, who had been placed at the head of the mutineers, had been killed by one of our rifle balls, and that a Subadar of one of the N.I. regiments, named Ghumander Singh, had been made leader; also that a boy of the Oudh royal family had been proclaimed king, and his mother, the Begum, regent.

After a short interval of rest Ungud again went forth. This time he took from Colonel Inglis to General Havelock despatches and plans showing our position and the roads leading to it; these being of great value, 5,000 rupees (£500) was promised to him if he succeeded in delivering them in safety.

Among those who had taken refuge in the Residency was Colonel Palmer, who had been major of brigade at Jullunder in 1846, and to whom I reported myself on my way to join my regiment. Shortly after the siege began his daughter lost her leg by a round shot which caused her death. She was sitting in the lower wing of the residency at the time; amputation was immediately performed, but she died on the next day. A few days after this date Major Francis, 13th N.I., received his death wound while sitting in the upper storey of the brigade mess by a round shot which fractured both his legs. He died next day after amputation. About this time Mr. M. C. Ommaney was wounded in the head by a round shot in the Redan Battery. The shot grazed his head and he lingered only for two days. By this time the casualties were very numerous, the hospital staff being greatly harassed. Among other things small-pox and cholera were raging among us, and in fact almost every ailment under the sun. Roughly speaking, the rebels besieging the garrison numbered not less than 150,000 at this time. Incessant firing of round shot and musketry went on day and night without ceasing, many bullets coming from a great distance. Again, many of the garrison were greatly hampered by finding their native servants continually deserting and joining the rebels; although none could get in, these could always find their way out. Provisions by this time were very scarce, and personally I had no regular meals, but got something to eat whenever I could. Grass was cut and boiled as a vegetable.

August had now arrived, bringing with it sore discouragement in the non-arrival of the promised relief, and producing great despondency in some of us. About this time the supply of tea and coffee failed among the soldiers, causing much privation. The laundry facilities were absolutely nil in the garrison; I was fortunate in possessing a flannel shirt. The strange part of this wearisome time was the monotony of each day and the difficulty of distinguishing Sunday from the rest, although throughout the siege divine services were carried on. After the death of the senior chaplain, Mr. Polehampton, the junior chaplain, Mr. Harris, performed the duty. Scouts were frequently sent out in quest of news of the relieving party, with little result. The enemy continued increasing their batteries, one twenty-four pounder doing specially great damage to my post, the church, the Residency, and the house at Innes's post, Lieutenant Innes's house from the outside being battered in, his verandah carried away, and the adjoining room on that side brought down. We counteracted this by placing an eighteen pounder of our own, which soon had the effect of silencing the enemy. One sad result of the firing from the twenty-four pounder named was the wounding of Ensign Studdy, 32nd Foot. This poor boy's injury was very remarkable; he was at the Residency in a centre room with several other officers, of whom I was one, when a round shot penetrated and struck him as he was crossing the room. Strangely enough in its passage it swept off the fringe of the punkah hanging there, which swathed his body round and round; it then struck him in the arm and chest, the wounds having the appearance of violent contusions. The arm was amputated and he died under the operation. On the 4th of August, during a high wind, a portion of the north-east wing of the Residency fell, burying six men of the 32nd, two of whom were extricated alive, the rest being killed. As there were no means of removing the *débris* their bodies remained here for a long time.

The Residency had been at this time vacated on account of its perilous condition, and the enemy soon discovered the fact. This had the effect of greatly increasing the firing upon the private houses. Most of these at this time were little short of wrecks and scarcely habitable, some of the occupants barely escaping with their lives from the falling masonry, notably Mr. W. C. Capper, C.S., and another, who were buried in the ruins, escaping miraculously.

On this same date, 10th August, a second general attack was made upon us; large bodies of the rebels had been seen moving about in the direction of the Cawnpore Road and crossing the river to our side, filling Johannes' house; here a mine was sprung by them about 11 A.M., greatly damaging an orphanage founded by a General Martinière, a Frenchman; the principal was Mr. Schilling, and all through the siege he and his boys rendered the greatest aid. The rooms occupied by them were by this mine explosion quite exposed; fortunately the room most destroyed was unoccupied at that moment. Mr. Schilling and his people had time to close the intervening doors, which alone now divided them from the rebels. After this the enemy began firing, when two soldiers, who had accompanied Brigadier Inglis to the scene of the disaster, were dangerously wounded by bullets passing through these door panels. The mutineers presently occupied all the buildings round about, and then began a desperate fusillade, their object being to take the Cawnpore Battery. In this they were again frustrated, being received by such a heavy fire of musketry from us that they fell back. At one moment some got so near that they were close upon the battery, hidden by a ditch, from which they were dislodged by hand-grenades.

While this was happening another mine was

being exploded by the rebels on the east side; this shattered some out-houses, where two European privates who were posted there had a miraculous escape, being blown into the air and falling to the ground uninjured; they regained the defences through a sharp fire from the enemy unhurt. Many other attacks were made, accompanied by mine explosions, the rebels advancing in great numbers, bringing scaling ladders to scale the south-west bastion. These again were dislodged by hand-grenades at the foot of the bastion; they were also very heavily fired upon; in their retreat they left on the road two of their dead, whom they were unable to remove; these bodies in a few days were completely stripped by jackals. In the afternoon the enemy again returned to the charge, this time making a sudden attack on the financial commissioner's office, commanded by Captain Sanders; here they became very bold, even seizing hold of the bayonets protruding from the loopholes; being again repulsed, they withdrew, keeping up a prolonged fire of musketry.

This was one of our busiest days; no less than 150 shells were used by us. In hand-to-hand work of this kind the hand-grenades were particularly serviceable, although care had to be shown in using them. They are in reality miniature shells, fired with a fuse in the same way; they are held in the hand, the fuse is ignited, and they are then thrown in the direction required at a particular moment. It can be understood that if the grenades are held a few moments too long in the hand they would burst, and cause great injury to the individual, as before related. We had again the satisfaction of knowing that the mutineers had received heavy losses throughout the day. Ours were as follows: three Europeans and two sepoys killed, and twelve men wounded.

And so the days wore on, amidst continual mining by the enemy and countermining by ourselves; in some instances the two parties working side by side and only divided by a wall. Frequently the rebels placed every form of obstruction in the way of our men, throwing brickbats, squibs, rockets, etc.; bamboos wrapped in oiled cloth were lighted and thrown, their object being to fire our men's outbuildings. One very successful effort on our part was made at 10 A.M. on the morning of the 11th of August. The garrison was warned that a mine was to be exploded; it was fired with great success, and brought the building occupied by the rebels down upon them, a number being killed. Many others were shot who ventured out to their aid. This gave great credit to the engineers who undertook the work. Nothing was more harassing at this time than the mining, that of the mutineers giving us great anxiety, whilst our own was attended with tremendous labour.

CHAPTER VI.

CONTINUATION OF SIEGE.

Ungud returns—Correspondence with General Havelock—Mining disaster—Attack on the breach—Sorties for destruction of out-buildings—Exploits of Browne, Fulton and McCabe—Removal of women to the Begum Kotee—New batteries of the enemy—An awkward mistake—Lieutenant Bonham's invention—A harmless little gamble—Fresh desertions—Removal of the powder magazine—Gallantry of Captain Fulton—Wild rumours—Prices current—Sickness and many deaths—Severe wound of Lieutenant Bonham.

OF all our messengers sent out Ungud was the only one who returned successfully. He re-appeared on the 15th of August bringing the following letter, of which I give a copy from Mr. Gubbins' History:—

"To M. GUBBINS, Esq.

"DEAR SIR,

"We march to-morrow morning for Lucknow, having been reinforced. We shall push on as speedily as possible. We hope to reach you in four days at furthest; *you must aid us in every way, even to cutting your way out, if we can't force our way in. We are only a small Force.* [1]

"(From General Havelock.)"

[1] N.B.—The words printed in italics were written in Greek characters.

Ungud arrived a fortnight after receiving this despatch, having been taken prisoner by the enemy, while endeavouring to reach us; the letter was concealed in a quill, sealed at the ends with wax, how kept from the enemy I cannot say, but when released, he again returned in search of the relieving force, wishing to obtain the latest intelligence. He discovered General Havelock's force, which, having been harassed by the Nana's men, had been obliged to retrace their steps, recrossing the river to Cawnpore, where the General was waiting for further reinforcements.

We afterwards learnt through Ungud that this force had achieved a victory over the rebels, but General Havelock had thought it expedient to return. Our conjectures were numerous as to what had caused this delay, but all felt convinced that it was to our advantage. Had the General understood the whole circumstances of our condition he would never have suggested the idea of cutting our way out, I am convinced; this being little short of suicide to all concerned, hampered as we were by many women, children, sick and wounded, our greatly reduced European force numbering 350 only, whilst our women 220, children 230, sick and wounded 120, and there were no means of carriage whatever. Again, our treasury contained 25 lacs (£250,000), to say nothing of the guns that would have been left behind; the sacrifice was not to be thought of.

Brigadier Inglis replied to this note in a lengthy

statement, representing our condition as being "urgent" and "desperate," especially from the provision point-of-view. The following reply was brought in by Ungud after a lapse of eleven days. I again quote Mr. Gubbins:—

"CAWNPORE,
"*August 24th.*

"MY DEAR COLONEL,

"I have your letter of the 16th inst. I can only say, do not *negotiate*, but rather perish, sword in hand. Sir Colin Campbell, who came out at a few days' notice to command, upon the news arriving of General Anson's death, promises me *fresh troops*, and you will be my first care. The re-inforcements may reach me in from *twenty to twenty-five days*, and I will prepare everything for a march on Lucknow.

"Yours very sincerely,
"H. HAVELOCK, Brig.-Gen.

"(TO COLONEL INGLIS, H.M. 32nd Regt.)"

By this letter we knew that the earliest date of our relief would be in about a month.

All this time the mining and countermining went on continuously, and at last the rebels succeeded in doing us real mischief by exploding a mine under the outer defences of the left Sheikh's square on the 18th of August. The explosion took place early in the morning, doing great damage to our buildings, and blowing up one of our posts, this outlook being kept by Lieutenant Masham, Captain

A. Orr and two sentries; Masham, Orr and one drummer were thrown into the air by the explosion, luckily descending inside the building, and escaped with little injury; the fourth, Band-Sergeant Curtin, of my regiment, was unfortunately blown outside and immediately killed; at the same time seven others —six bandsmen and a sepoy—were all killed inside the building.

This gave the mutineers what they required, *viz.*, a breach in the wall nearly fourteen feet long, through which they began to stream; the leader, mounting the wall, waved his sword, but was at once struck down by a bullet fired by an officer from the brigade mess; a second attempted the ascent, but shared the same fate. After this they contented themselves by firing from their own shelters on this breach. At once every man was at his post, and the 84th was told off to barricade this weak spot; after working desperately all night, this was completed, the brigadier himself superintending the operations. Our losses were several wounded, and here, through a loophole, Mon. Duprât received his death-wound from one of the enemy's bullets.

All this rendered it necessary that a sortie should be made to destroy outbuildings which were by this time much too near our own, and had it been done before it would have spared us much annoyance and saved many lives. Johannes' house was especially in this category. Brigadier Inglis himself, accompanied by Captain Fulton and other engineers, occupied all these houses without trouble; they then blew up the buildings with gunpowder. Repeated sorties went on till all were demolished.

On the 21st inst. we had our revenge for the mischief done by the mine exploded by the rebels. Captain Fulton planned the measure, and Lieutenant Innis aided him untiringly; for sixty hours he scarcely rested. We succeeded in demolishing the house of Mr. Johannes (senior) and the tower from which the marksmen had done us so much harm. These men were known as the African Riflemen, their aim being very deadly. In the *débris* many of the enemy were buried.

Yet another sortie was as follows: a number of Europeans, fifty in all, divided into two parties, one under Lieutenant Browne, 32nd, reached a battery where they found a gunner of the enemy sleeping securely upon one of the guns. Lieutenant Browne proceeded to snap his revolver at him, but unsuccessfully; he then awoke and bolted. An attempt was then made to spike the guns, but ineffectually; the touch-holes had become enlarged by repeated use; and the annoying part was that within four hours these very guns were again at work upon the brigade mess. Lieutenant Browne for his action here received the Victoria Cross. Meanwhile the other party under Fulton and McCabe reached Johannes' shop verandah. Fulton, finding the doors of the building closed, placed his back against one, and, thrusting his feet against the verandah wall forced the frame of the door out of the masonry, falling backwards into the room which was full of the rebels. The room was intersected with deep trenches, dug to protect from shells; into one of these he fell backwards. Immediately McCabe and his party followed, the enemy fled, and the whole buildings were then blown up with two barrels of gunpowder, by means of a slow match.

In all, our casualties in these operations were three killed and two wounded. Many more mining attacks upon us followed, but were met and successfully foiled in every instance but the one previously related. No words of praise can do justice to that indefatigable officer, Captain Fulton, and all the engineers concerned in these operations. The rebels attempted to set fire to the gates at the Bailey Guard; in this also they were frustrated. By this time most of our buildings were hardly habitable, and the Residency was so perforated with round shot that it was considered unsafe even for stores. The brigade mess, guard houses and judicial garrison house were all in a state of collapse; so unsafe were they that it was considered prudent to remove the women from these into the Begum Kotee.

The rebels were continually opening fresh batteries upon us, some doing much damage, and all proving fresh sources of danger in our now battered condition. They constructed these batteries with marvellous skill and cunning, showing that our lessons given them had not been thrown away.

On one occasion they had succeeded in placing a twenty-four pounder and a twelve pounder in a very advantageous position, and these they fired in quick succession, the result being that a breach was made in our wall of defence. Whilst Brigadier Inglis came to inspect it, and we had all congregated within a bastion close by, the rebels, perceiving this, opened fire upon us, the result being that two of us were killed: Lieutenant Webb, of the 32nd, and a poor sweeper named Lalloo. The bastion was speedily evacuated, and the brigadier sent orders to the Mortar Battery to shell the enemy at a distance of 200 yards. A mistake in this order nearly cost the lives of Major Apthorp and Captain Edgell. Lieutenant Cunliffe passed the order on to the sergeant who, mistaking it, charged the mortar with an insufficient quantity of powder; thus, the shell fell among ourselves instead of outside!

About this period an admirable and efficient invention was made by Lieutenant Bonham, Artillery. This consisted of firing a mortar horizontally instead of vertically as hitherto. The mortar was mounted on a carriage which we called the "ship," and proved of excellent service. This gallant young officer had frequently shown the greatest bravery, and had been wounded at Chinhut; he had also shown great bravery on the outbreak of the Mutiny at Secrora.

During the Mutiny any authentic news of the mutineers was rewarded by money, not by any stated sum, the applicant being allowed to put his hand into a bag of rupees and take out as many as he could with one hand. It was diverting to watch him; he was allowed three tries; first he would bring out his hand closed on as many as he could hold, looking at them, he thought he could better this, so putting them back he would bring out his hand open, with as much as he could manage to bring out of the bag. After all the sum was not very large, but the little "gamble" appealed to them.

Still we were without intelligence of the relieving force. This fact produced great uneasiness among ourselves, and what almost amounted to panic among the natives. It occasioned fresh desertions, one native artilleryman deserting in broad daylight, also an Eurasian and ten Christian drummers who had been in the King of Oudh's service. One cannot be surprised at their going when it is remembered that they were half natives and all their relations were among the rebels outside.

The position of our gunpowder magazine, by this time the most precious of our possessions, being considered unsafe, it was found necessary to remove it—a difficult task; for, having been stored outside the residency, it was now unpleasantly near the enemy. This work completed gave us all much satisfaction, as it was now placed underground in the Begum Kotee. It was now discovered that the rebels were mining around us in all directions, and their endeavours would have been successful, but for the heroic efforts of Captain Fulton and Lieutenant Hutchinson (Engineers), the former being especially brave in counter-mining and following the enemy into their own passage. Sufficient justice can never be done to these brave officers, more particularly to Captain Fulton. This gallant man must have suffered terribly from heat during this period, spending many hours underground each day in the terrible heat of the month of August. There is no doubt but that under Providence the Lucknow garrison at this period owed its safety to his perseverance, boldness and skill.

The natives affected to disbelieve the goings and comings of Ungud, and persisted in stating to the others their belief that he was kept in hiding by us in the meantime. We knew that some of the natives in the garrison were in communication with the rebels, as Ungud, who moved among the enemy, discovered that our movements were all known to them. The wildest rumours reached us, among others that the natives in our midst were planning a plot by which they meant to attack all Europeans at a given signal, and simultaneously the rebels were to be allowed by them to enter and so annihilate us; the origin of this we never discovered.

The month of August was drawing to a close, and in consequence of many deaths of officers among us frequent sales were taking place of their effects. I quote some of the prices, which ranged as follows:

Brandy £16 per dozen (before the siege ended as much as £2 10s. was given for a bottle), sherry £7 per dozen, and cigars 2s. each (these rose to 5s. each).

Sickness was again very rife among us, the victims being many children; also the deaths took place of Dr. MacDonald, of my regiment, 41st N. I., from cholera, and Lieutenant Bryce from the same disease, the latter after recovering from a very severe wound.

The chief engineer, Major J. Anderson, died after much suffering, principally from fatigue and exhaustion, also Captain Barlow, my companion in the vestry, and Mrs. Greene, wife of Captain Greene, 48th N. I. Among the deaths were 125 privates of the 32nd and 48th Regiments, who had all either been killed or died from their wounds during this month. Captain Power, 32nd, died from his wound, and a clerk named "Wales" had been killed. Among the wounded were: Captain Waterman, 13th N. I.; Lieutenant James Alexander, Artillery; Lieutenant Fletcher, 48th N. I.; Lieutenant J. Cunliffe, Artillery; Mr. MacRae, Engineering Department; Captain Hawes, and, lastly, Lieutenant Bonham, to whom we owed so much, was severely wounded for the third time by a musket ball which struck him on the breast and broke the collar-bone, thus placing this brave fellow, who could be ill spared at this period, *hors de combat* for the remainder of the siege.

CHAPTER VII.

INCIDENTS DURING THE SIEGE

Cooler weather—A fatal oversight—Explosion near the south-western bastion—Attacks redoubled—Continued mining and countermining—Disastrous result of misplaced economy—Death of Captain Fulton—Instance of his intrepidity—Magnitude of our loss—Promotion of Lieutenant J. C. Anderson—Rajah Man Singh—Desertion of cooks—Further dilapidation of buildings—More of the horizontal mortar—Heavy losses among the Artillery—Effect of an eclipse—Further casualties—The problem of dress and laundry.

We now came to the month of September, when the weather was dry, and the nights and mornings were becoming cooler. We hoped the rainy season was over, but about the third week in this month we experienced an absolute deluge of rain, doing harm to our defences, adding greatly to our discomforts, and hindering Havelock's last advance. On September 2nd a most regrettable accident occurred. A party of four Engineer officers, one of whom was Lieutenant Birch, who was then attached to this branch (he was a son of my old commanding officer and escaped with me from Seetapore), went out at dusk to examine the spot of a suspected mine; and the usual warning was given to all posts in the vicinity, with the exception of one by an oversight. They had accomplished their task and were returning, when the sentry at this post, seeing figures moving in the dark, mistook them for the enemy and fired, mortally wounding poor Birch in the abdomen; he died during the night in great agony. His sister and his wife, to whom he had been married but six months, were in Lucknow with him. Yet another calamity! This was the death of Major Bruere, who commanded the 13th N. I.; he was killed on the 4th of this month by a rifle ball penetrating the chest. He was an excellent marksman, and, whilst engaged in firing from the brigade mess, he unfortunately exposed himself too much. All the days of this month the enemy continued their work of mining unceasingly; and, in addition, cannonading and firing of musketry would begin at daybreak, continuing for about three hours, and then again resumed in the afternoon with still greater vehemence.

At this time no less than five mines were known by us to be in course of construction, one of them planned against my late post in the church; and, in addition to this number, the large one constructed against the Redan Battery still existed. On September 5th the garrison received a great scare by the explosion of a mine in close proximity to our most important bastion, *viz.*, the south-western. We had suspected that this bastion was being mined, but we could not be sure. The explosion occurred about

10 A.M., and was a terrific one; the fallen *débris*, smoke, and closeness of the noise gave every one the impression that this stronghold had gone, and that with it must follow the garrison. So imagine our delight on finding the bastion still intact and realising that the firing, though close, had not been near enough to accomplish the deed. The mutineers had, however, effected a large fissure and caused great damage to the houses near, and they followed up the explosion by promptly fixing to the walls a huge ladder with double rungs; but this we never allowed them to scale, for as fast as their muzzles appeared at the embrasure they were met by Major Apthorp and the men of the 32nd with hand-grenades and musket-shots, whilst all in the background kept up a heavy fire from the loopholes with which most buildings were now pierced. After an engagement of an hour and a half, they fell back with great loss. Our losses were three killed and one wounded.

As the time approached for the relieving force to be getting near, the enemy became more and more persistent, convincing us that they too knew this fact. Attacks became almost continuous, but by this period we had well learnt the lesson of defence, and every effort of theirs was repulsed, frequently with great loss on their side. About this time they directed their attention upon the hospital and near buildings, an eighteen pounder gun being directed on the former, and, strange to say, a shot from this gun passed down the whole length of the ward, crowded with patients, without any one sustaining harm!

By this time the whole of the garrison was a network of mines, and wherever we had discovered traces of the enemy's mining we had met them with counter-mining, numbers being destroyed by us in this way. Frequently we could hear the cries and groans of the rebels buried in the ruins.

One day a sortie was made, under Captain Fulton, to examine the shaft and gallery of a mine which had been discovered in the churchyard. A long gallery was discovered, directed against the church, and of sufficient height to allow a man walking along it almost erect; this was destroyed with gunpowder.

As before stated, our south-west bastion was considered by us all as our weak point, being opposed by four guns of the rebels, two very heavy ones and two lighter. Major Apthorp, who commanded this post, had pointed out from the first the necessity of silencing these guns, but so far it had not been done, from fear that by so doing we should give the enemy the use of our round shot (as I must here mention that they fired this upon us again); only an occasional fire, therefore, was kept up, an Artillery officer visiting the post for two hours every day, firing a shot every twenty minutes. These few shots produced little effect upon either of the rebel batteries, whilst the enemy used theirs upon us to such purpose that great work was necessary to keep up repairs which were mostly carried out at night.

This economy of shot was destined to cost us very dearly—the life of that most brilliant, resourceful and gifted man, Captain Fulton. It happened as follows: Major Apthorp, having at last obtained permission to keep up a continuous cannonade, Lieutenant J. Alexander, Artillery, was appointed to carry this into effect. He was most successful, and after some twenty shots succeeded in blowing the rebels' embrasure to pieces, also damaging the carriage of a twenty-four pounder gun; this the enemy deserted, and it was never again put into action against us. Later in the day poor Fulton went to examine the effect of Alexander's cannonade. While scrutinising the battered embrasure through his glasses, and finding some of the enemy at work there, he called to Alexander to come up and continue firing, he himself leading the way. At the moment when we reached the embrasure one of the guns directed upon our garden battery opened fire; the ball striking Captain Fulton carried off the top of his head, his death being instantaneous. Thus, at almost the close of our siege, this distinguished man was taken from us. He had ever been foremost in the fighting, and his loss to us all was irreparable. He had constantly placed himself in the face of the greatest danger in order to effect his purpose and to shield his men. An instance I will here relate showing his disregard of danger. A few days previous to his death he had made a sortie in order to destroy a house which commanded Innes' shattered post which was being loopholed by the enemy. Captain Fulton and his men succeeded in scaling a wall by a ladder, taking two barrels of gunpowder which they placed near the building; he then bade the soldiers "retire"; he fired the train and hastened to the ladder, only to find his men thoughtlessly loitering; he immediately returned to them and hastened them up the ladder; but, before he could follow, the mine exploded. He had a marvellous escape, for, although the wall blown up was within ten feet of him, a slight contusion caused by a piece of falling wood was his only injury.

Readers of the epitome of this great man's doings will have formed an estimate of our loss. Although it was upon every individual's exertions during this trying time that our safety depended, upon none rested such responsibility as on Captain Fulton. Mr. Gubbins rightly designated him "The Defender of Lucknow". I never heard, but I only trust that the Government of that day did not neglect to do honour to his survivors, as he left a widow and a large family of children inadequately provided for.

Two days after this tragedy the Garden Battery that occasioned it was reduced to ruins by a few shots from us. Lieutenant J. C. Anderson, Madras Engineers, succeeded Captain Fulton as chief of the Engineering Department; he had already given us many proofs of his suitability for this post.

About this time the infamous rebel and taloodar, Rajah Man Singh, joined the rest of them outside Lucknow, thinking that Havelock had abandoned us and that our case was hopeless. Ungud discovered when he recrossed the Ganges that Man Singh had levied heavy taxes on the merchants of Fyzabad in order to join mutineers. This man was a reputed soldier, and, although not one of the oldest of the Oudh chiefs, he had been a power at the Court of the King in Lucknow, and had given much trouble to the British residents. Among the natives his influence was considerable, and his history one of rapacity. He had great caste influence, as he had placed himself at the head of the Hindoos in a fanatical rising which was waged against the Mohammedans during the years 1854 and 1855.

More desertions of natives took place about this time, and among others the cooks of the Artillery and 32nd Regiment deserted, at the time causing great inconvenience. The ruins of the buildings became more complete during this month; walls were frequently breached and had to be replaced by stockades.

Innes' house fell in at this period (nearly burying the sentries in the ruins) and had to be abandoned; not a building was there in our whole line of defence but showed great signs of delapidation.

The invention constructed by Lieutenant Bonham, before mentioned, was used with much success, being brought to bear when no other weapon was of use. A second ship was constructed, and brought into use with equal effect upon the enemy's batteries. Major Simons, C.O.A., died on the 8th, having never recovered from his wounds received at Chinhut. His death was followed on the 22nd by that of Lieutenant Foster Cunliffe, also of the Artillery, whose death was caused by low fever. He had long been exposed in his successful guard of the Redan Battery. He was engaged to a young lady in the garrison. We had now lost nearly all the Artillery officers, either from death or wounds; four were dead and four wounded; one, Captain Thomas, alone escaped, but he, too, was greatly shattered in health. At the outset we were weak in this branch, and mainly upon their exertions our safety had depended. A weird effect was caused by an eclipse on the 18th; everywhere was almost total darkness. It lasted for three hours, to the great consternation of the rebels; nothing was heard from them during this period. Apthorp, who took particular note of the enemy at this time, said they all appeared to be in hiding, not knowing what was coming next! Not a shot was fired.

Besides the casualties named, we lost three other officers in September. Lieutenant James Graham, 4th Light Cavalry, whilst distracted by the strain, threw himself off one of the buildings. (To digress somewhat, I have by me a portrait of this poor fellow's twin daughters, born in Lucknow at this period, very beautiful girls.) Captain Mansfield,

32nd Regiment, died from cholera; also Lieutenant Fullerton, who had been Assistant Commissioner at Duriabad, died in hospital. Ensign Hewitt, 41st N.I., was wounded about this time. The paucity of clothing among us had long been a source of great discomfort. Most of us began the siege with only what we were clothed in; from various causes nearly all had lost everything at the outset. With some of us our condition was very piteous, as we were veritably reduced to rags. A notable exception during this period was Captain Barwell, who, to the admiration and puzzlement of the rest of us, managed to turn out each day well groomed and laundried—how, we never knew! How fortunate it was in this respect that it had been the hot season, or cold would have been added to our inflictions.

CHAPTER VIII.

FURTHER INCIDENTS.

News from Sir James Outram—Welcome sound of artillery—Death of Captain Radcliffe—Flight of the enemy—Arrival of the relieving force—Demonstrations of joy—Losses by the way—Eager enquiries—Delafosse and Thompson among the arrivals—Straitened commissariat—The new tobacco—Lieutenant Moorsom—Death of Neill and Cooper—Details of Havelock's advance—Outram's magnanimity—Recipients of the V.C.—Deaths by sorties—Total losses, European and native—Case of Colonel Birch—Of Graves—Outram in command—Second phase of the siege, the blockade—Successful work by Colonel Napier—Rewards to Ungud and other natives—Discontent of our own men—Unwholesome food—Tantalising position of our stores—Distress and mortality among the wounded—News of the capture of Delhi.

On the 22nd Ungud returned to garrison, bringing good news from General Sir James Outram. We learnt that a fully equipped army was now approaching Lucknow, having crossed the Ganges on the 19th. "God grant that it may soon reach us," was the prayer on each one's lips. The general advised our making no attempt to aid their force, unless such as could be done "in perfect safety". Thus was Havelock's promise entirely carried out, the force crossing the river one day later only. Never did glad tidings fly so quickly, and never did any news bring such joy and thankfulness as this!

On 23rd September, the distant sound of artillery in the direction of Cawnpore was distinctly heard, and still nearer and nearer as the day advanced came the welcome sounds, convincing us that Havelock's force was now fighting with the mutineers outside. Ungud was almost beside himself with delight. Here was convincing proof! He exclaimed: "Dekho Fouj ata hai!" (See! Our troops are coming!)

The next day the sounds were much less audible, creating a little concern among us, more especially among the natives, as the terrible possibility of a repulse could not but force itself upon one. During the night of the 24th, Captain Radcliffe, 7th Cavalry, met with what proved to be his death wound, being hit by a round shot while on duty in the Cawnpore Battery; besides a broken arm, he received internal injuries, these proving fatal. This was a great loss of a most distinguished officer, who, at the defeat of Chinhut had saved absolute disaster by rallying his few volunteer cavalry at the critical moment; and now, with the *sound of relief* so near, he succumbed.

Sept. 25th.—A sepoy crossed our lines with a note from General Outram; it was dated the 16th, and gave us only the repeated assurance that he was approaching. The messenger soon left with the brigadier's reply; he could add nothing beyond that the force had reached the outskirts of the city. The heavy firing now heard gave great joy; then about 11.30 A.M. the firing ceased, and numbers of the city people could be seen flying over the bridges across the river, laden with their "goods and chattels". Later on the stampede was in full force, sepoys, sowars and matchlock men all fleeing for their lives, aided by every shot that we could fire after them as a parting farewell, a cross fire being kept up, as the rebels assailed us by a perfect hurricane of shot and shell from all their batteries. About 2 P.M. smoke from our guns was visible; a little later the rattle of musketry could be heard; by 4 P.M. those on the tower could clearly distinguish European troops and officers in movement; and by 5 P.M. the rumble of artillery reached us, and joy of joys! there were the 78th Highlanders and the Sikhs, charging up the main street, leading to the residency, fighting desperately as they came; and there, too, was General Outram, before one could give voice to a cheer, dismounting near the Bailey Guard Gate. Thus was the long-expected, long-hoped for, among us, and there followed an indescribable scene of delight; cheers broke forth from every post, trench, battery, and behind every sand bag, while even the inmates of the hospital crawled forth to join in this outburst of cheering in honour of those who had suffered so much to reach us; and thus, after being beaten back three times, they succeeded in fighting their way through and reaching us. If they had not arrived when they did, we should have lost the sepoys who stood by us so well, men of the regiment who had formed the Lucknow Force. It was indeed a relief, and ever grateful shall we feel to that force for their heroic efforts, for nothing but the greatest determination on their part could have succeeded in reaching the residency.

As the soldiers entered through the Bailey Guard Gate the enthusiasm was unbounded, the Highlanders greeting the garrison like joyous children. At the house of Dr. Fayrer, where the ladies and children were congregated, the bearded Highlanders rushed to clasp the ladies' hands; they took the children in their arms and fondly caressed them, passing them from one to the other to be caressed in turn. After this scene of indescribable delight, they sadly reflected one with another upon the losses they had sustained, of the many comrades who had fallen on the way. From the day they crossed the Ganges, 19th September, up to the 25th, the day they reached us, their total loss in killed and wounded, officers and men, was 535. All honour and praise therefore to the relieving force.

As the evening wore on the excitement increased; one can imagine how anxiously relations and friends were inquired after. For 113 days no post had been received, and no communication with the outer world had taken place. Whilst some sought for dear ones in the relieving force, others anxiously inquired how it was with Delhi, Agra, Cawnpore, etc., and news of the world at large was eagerly asked for. Among the arrivals was Lieutenant Delafosse, who with Mowbray Thompson were the sole survivors of the Cawnpore massacre. They succeeded in swimming down the Ganges and so escaped.

I remember perfectly well serving out beer to the new arrivals until I felt overpowered by the fumes. By degrees we quieted down, and the garrison went to sleep with a feeling of security that they had not known for many weeks. After their arrival with regard to provisions we were rather worse off than before, as all the supplies brought with them had been left at the Alum Bagh, from which we were cut off. Tobacco was much wanted, tea-leaves and leaves from bushes were dried and smoked, but I can't say there was much satisfaction in them; an old pipe was supposed to give them a flavour of tobacco, but not that of which a connoisseur would approve!

Another of those who came in with the relieving force was Lieutenant Moorsom, to whom we owed much, for he had been selected in 1856 by the Commissioners of Lucknow to make a scientific survey of the city, and it was owing to his excellent plans, then made of a large portion of the city surrounding the residency, that success attended so many of our efforts. Lieutenant Moorsom was in Calcutta at the time General Havelock's staff was being formed, and fortunately he was placed upon it. His aid and personal knowledge were of the greatest assistance, both in bringing this force in and also in guiding in the second column of Havelock's army, and again upon other occasions when sorties had to be made.

Among other details we learnt that General Neill, a fine soldier, had lost his life in fighting his way through the mutineers, whilst effecting an entrance into the city the previous day, as also an old friend of mine, Brigadier Cooper, whom I had known at Ajmere in '47; that Deputy-Quartermaster-General Lieutenant-Colonel B. Fraser Tytler was badly wounded; and that General Havelock's son also was known to be seriously wounded, but had not yet come in. Even now many had not entered the garrison, as they were engaged fighting their way inch by inch with different rebel forces. None of the big guns had yet appeared.

By degrees we learnt of the difficulties that Havelock's army had met with, from their earliest efforts to reach us. They had fought five pitched battles, and been obliged to make three retreats owing to the small force available. They had crossed the Ganges on the 25th of July with a force of 1,500 only; Havelock fought two battles on the 29th, defeating the rebels, but suffering heavy losses. In addition to this, cholera was raging amongst this small army. These causes necessitated a retreat to Mungulwar on the 31st, where he procured slight reinforcements, and again took the offensive, but with a force of 1,400 only, this time encountering and defeating the enemy at Busheergunje. Whilst resting after this action he received a despatch from Lord Canning, telling him of the mutiny of the Dinapore Brigade, up to that time supposed to be coming to his aid; also that no reinforcements could be sent for some time.

This would almost have daunted any but a Havelock; no wonder that for the time being he decided to retrace his footsteps, feeling almost assured that the relief of the Lucknow garrison was under the circumstances an impossibility. And yet, by August 6th, this indomitable man with his handful of men had again occupied Mungulwar, and was constructing a bridge of boats across the Ganges to Cawnpore, for his force to cross over again; at the same time he put ample defences to protect his men against any attack from the enemy, thus becoming in easier touch with Cawnpore. On the 11th with a force of 1,000 men, Havelock took the road a third time for Lucknow. This time success again followed them, the enemy fleeing from their guns, which he captured, returning with them to Mungulwar. On the 13th and 16th of August other engagements followed. The last of these ended General Havelock's first great efforts for the relief of Lucknow, under difficulties greater than any general had ever encountered. Although resting at Cawnpore for a month after these exertions, preparations were made for the next move. This rest the soldiers were terribly in need of.

By the 16th of September the reinforcements

arrived, commanded by General Outram, and it was then decided to make a rapid start. This officer, with rare magnanimity, waived his claim to the command in order that General Havelock should have all the merit of the relief. They marched out a total force of 3,179, arriving on the 25th of September, as already related.

For gallant deeds performed during the entry into Lucknow, the following received the V.C.: Captain Olpherts (afterwards Sir William, known in the army as "Hell-fire Jack"), Surgeon-Major Jee, and the adjutant, Lieutenant Macpherson, of the 78th Highlanders, who led them in a brilliant charge.

The enemy having now removed their guns to a greater distance, some of their shots did more damage than before, as when they were close they went over the entrenchment, while now they fell inside.

During the sorties made since the relief many valuable lives were lost. The following are the names of some of the officers, who either were killed or died from their wounds at this time: Captain Hughes, 57th N. I.; Lieutenant D. Alexander, Artillery; Captain McCabe, 32nd Regiment; Major Simmons, 5th Fusiliers; and Mr. F. D. Lucas, an Irish gentleman who was travelling in India at the outbreak and joined the Lucknow garrison at the beginning of the siege. In consequence of an ammunition waggon laden with our letters and newspapers having been left at the Alum Bagh, few of us received any of these until the final relief on November 17th.

Our total European loss up to this was 350 killed, and of natives 133; as many as 230 deserted —a total loss in all of 713, from a garrison originally 1692 strong, *viz.*, Europeans 927, natives 765. We had lost during the siege forty-one military and two civil officers and one assistant chaplain.

Since the day the regiment mutinied events had followed so quickly that at the time the loss of so many old friends was hardly realised; one seemed to be in some terrible dream. It was scarcely credible that a whole army which had done so much was gone; disappeared, as far as the Company's army could be reckoned, but now struggling for existence as a herd of rebels thirsting for blood. Although the same question could be asked in every case, I could not conceive why they should have taken Colonel Birch's life. A more considerate commanding officer there could not have been; a master of the language, and perfectly acquainted with all their prejudices, one would have thought there were some at least in the regiment who would have protected him. I lost a good friend, one to whom I was greatly indebted for much kindness. In 1854, when studying for an examination in Hindustani, he gave me great help, corrected my exercises and improved my pronunciation, with the result that I passed, the only one that did so out of three that went up. It was good to see the old man's delight when the result was known.

Poor Graves, too, our adjutant was another case. They tried to kill him, but only wounded him; eventually he died of cholera in the residency. I think he took the Mutiny to heart more than any one I knew. He thought that he had so thoroughly obtained the men's confidence that they would have given him warning beforehand of what was going to happen; and to find out in the end that all they told him was false, was more than he could bear. *He was a good adjutant and had great pride in the regiment.* This, and having no news of his father, who commanded a brigade at Delhi, so affected him that when attacked by cholera he succumbed at once.

Sir James Outram now assumed the command, making his headquarters at Dr. Fayrer's house, whilst General Havelock resided at the late Mr. Ommaney's. Although the various posts covered an extent of over two miles, General Havelock accomplished this round every morning shortly after daybreak. Brigadier Inglis retained charge of the survivors of the old garrison, both military and civil, and in addition a few of the relieving force; General Havelock, of what was then called the Oudh Field Force, composed of most of the newly arrived troops. Thus another phase of the siege began, this time called "a blockade".

The united forces were not considered sufficiently

strong to fight their way out, hampered as they were by the wounded, women and children, so another period of waiting commenced for still further relief. Day by day the same tactics went on as before the 25th, only that now we were enabled to become much stronger in all our defences, many of them proving an unparalleled success. Chief and foremost among our engineers at this time was Colonel Napier, afterwards to become Lord Napier of Magdala.

Amongst those rewarded by Sir J. Outram was Ungud; for his faithful services he received in cash £1,500, being £500 for each despatch brought in by him, thus becoming, for a native of his class, a rich man, which he thoroughly deserved. Many other rewards were likewise given at this time, but almost entirely to the native force, these being fully satisfied. Not so our own men, who grumbled considerably at the want of recognition of their services. Most of them comforted themselves with the reflection that this would come later on; to my knowledge this further recognition has never been made. Here is an instance of what I mean: for services during the siege Europeans received one year's service, whilst natives received two years' service, towards pensions.

Now, as before, bread was unknown among us. No bakers accompanied Havelock; chupatties constituted our staple food. With many these did not agree, but produced dysentery and diarrhœa; personally I rather liked them, but then they agreed with me. It is probable that this led to the death of our rescuer, General Havelock, later on, the need of nourishing food being much felt; no green vegetables nor food of this kind could be procured, and this greatly increased all diseases of a scrofulous nature during the blockade. It was tantalising to know that stores for us, detained at the Alum Bagh, comprised tea, coffee, sugar, rum, wine, spirits and even tobacco. Clothing, in addition, was all stored within four miles of us; it might have been a thousand for all the good it was.

To add to our discomfort the cold increased, as we were closely approaching the cold season; and our clothing was of the scantiest, most of us possessing only what we stood upright in. This may sound trivial, but let any of my readers try the experiment of being restricted to one suit of clothing during six months, and he will the better realise our discomfort. The distress among the wounded in hospital was most pitiable: they were terribly crowded; comforts were almost unobtainable; most of the invalid diet had been used. Needless to say, great mortality was the result, even among those slightly wounded, gangrene being frequently one of the causes, and all this in spite of the almost superhuman efforts of the medical men to alleviate suffering.

Among those dying at this time were Mr. Cameron, of the original Garrison, Captain Denison, 9th Light Infantry, and Captain L'Estrange, 5th Fusiliers, the last-named a hero of the celebrated

"Arrah" defence. A singular accident befel a private of the Madras Fusiliers: he had fallen down a well, and was discovered still alive, three days after, by a reconnoitring party that had been sent out to take a battery. On October 3rd Major Haliburton was mortally wounded whilst leading the 78th Highlanders in an engagement with the rebels; Major Stephenson, Madras Fusiliers, and several other officers were wounded about the same time, Major Stephenson afterwards dying from his wound; and Lieutenant G. W. Greene died from dysentery.

On October 9th the good news reached us of the capture of Delhi, and the march of Brigadier Greathead towards Oudh commenced. This gave us all great joy, and again the loyal natives were encouraged.

A fellow cadet of mine at Addiscombe, Captain Graydon, 44th N. I., was killed by a musket ball on the 28th.

CHAPTER IX.

ARRIVAL OF RELIEVING FORCE.

Mr. Kavanagh's plucky feat—Casualties from recklessness—Death of Colonel Campbell—Approach of the relieving force observed—Fighting at the Sekundur Bagh—Taking of the Shah Nujeef—Captain Wolseley plants the British ensign—Strength and casualties of Sir Colin Campbell's force—Evacuation of the Residency—My Arab in a palkee-gharry—Terrible experience of Captain Waterman—Removal of the treasury—Our six months' mail—A treasured piece of furniture—Honour for General Havelock—His death—Wisdom of Sir Colin's arrangements—A youthful thief—A novel experience—Arrival at Cawnpore—Kindness of two officers—Irate Mrs. Apthorp—Christmas Day—Mrs. Halford again—Reception at Calcutta—Lady Canning's kindness—Ladies of the garrison sail in the *Ava*—Wrecked off Trincomalee—Effect of the calamity—Fifteen months' leave—A strange greeting—Voyage back to India—Thirteen brides to be—Incident at Suez—An exacting charge—"Devils and devils"—An exciting drive.

A RUMOUR now reached us that a relieving force under the commander-in-chief himself was on its way to our rescue; whereupon the general despatched a messenger to Alum Bagh with plans of the city, and advice as to its approach, and how best to effect a junction with us. Fortunately this messenger reached the Alum Bagh in safety. Mr. Kavanagh at this time volunteered to go out to the chief's camp and guide him through the city. Mr. Kavanagh was a civilian in one of the commissioner's offices, and it was plucky of him to make the offer; he disguised himself in native dress, and accompanied by a native left the entrenchment at night, swam the Goomtee, and eventually succeeded in reaching the chief's camp, for which he afterwards received the V. C., £2,000, and the post of assistant commissioner in the Indian Civil Service.

On November 4th Ensign Dashwood, 48th N. I., contrary to all advice, insisted upon sketching in an exposed part of the residency grounds, when a round shot passed close by him, and narrowly missed him. This was followed shortly by another, which took off both his legs. During this day four more casualties occurred, the others being two of the 32nd and two of the 35th, all from the same cause, *viz.*, reckless exposure!

November 13th.—Colonel Campbell, C.B., died from the after-result of amputation of his leg. He, like so many others, had not strength to bear the operation.

November 14th.—The advance of the relieving force is clearly visible from the heights, and after dark beacons are lighted by them to show that they are in possession of the Dilkoosha and Martinière. Still the enemy does not cease its activity. Musketry fire continues throughout the night.

The days of the 15th and 16th were passed by all of us in watching from various heights all that could be seen of the doings of the advancing column, but it was only afterwards that we heard the following details of the fighting on the 16th at the Sekundur Bagh, which was at this time an enclosed square surrounded by a high wall of solid masonry. The mutineers had made this square into a defence, and loopholed the wall, and now a fearful fire of musketry began upon our advancing men; whereupon the infantry lay down till the guns had effected a breach wide enough for three or four to enter abreast. Then the 93rd Highlanders most heroically stormed it, and after discharging their rifles followed up with the bayonet. The first man through this breach was, I believe, Captain Burroughs, of the 93rd, an old school-fellow of mine at Blackheath Proprietary School. The front entrance was then forced, when the 53rd Foot, 4th Punjabees and the detachments of other regiments entered, led by Major Barnston. Here followed a terrible retribution. Within this enclosure were found some 2,000 rebels, all of whom, with the exception of two or three, were annihilated by our forces. Many went down on their knees begging for "quarter," but none was given, most of them being bayoneted.

In taking the Shah Nujeef the same detachments, again led by Major Barnston, met with a desperate resistance. A company of the 93rd, which was well in advance, was met by a terrible fire when within fifteen yards of the principal building, and whilst searching for the entrance both subalterns were wounded, Lieutenant E. C. Wynne and Ensign

H. Powell. Thereupon the men fell back, Major Barnston, hastening to bring up the rest, was wounded by a shell from one of our own guns. He died afterwards at Cawnpore from the effects; a sad fate for this brave fellow! After this sad occurrence, the commander-in-chief caused the heavy guns to cease firing for two hours. He then allowed the 93rd Highlanders to endeavour to take the building. This was not possible till Brigadier Hope had sent for a twenty-four pounder from H.M.S. *Shannon*, brought up by Captain Peel, the sailors and the Highlanders dragging it close up to the building, under a heavy musketry fire. Still great obstacles were met with, as after a breach had been effected in the outer wall an inner one was discovered, while the intense smoke and dust caused by this heavy cannonade greatly impeded the work. All this time the enemy were keeping up a heavy fire from an elevated position, in spite of the rifles of the 93rd. At this juncture Captain Peel noted a tree which commanded a good vantage over the enemy, and immediately offered the V.C. to any man volunteering to climb it. Three men at once started to make the ascent. They were Lieutenants N. Salmon and Southwall, and Harrison (leading seaman). Lieutenant Southwall was killed, the others being wounded. The mutineers, becoming alarmed by this time, fled, and, the Highlanders rushing in at the breach, the Shah Nujeef was ours.

November 17.—By 9.30 A.M. we were convinced

that Sir Colin's forces were in full activity, as they were bombarding the 32nd mess house, which afterwards proved to be abandoned by the rebels; upon this we also concentrated our full energies; the men of the *Shannon* brought a heavy gun closely to bear upon the mess house, amidst an unusual fire from the mutineers, who were mounted on the roof of the Tara Kotta and adjoining buildings, and in a short time the destruction was complete. By 3 P.M. the red coats were seen steadily advancing towards the building, headed by an officer who entered first, and through our glasses we shortly perceived a man upon the roof; this proved to be Captain Wolseley, 90th Regiment (now Field-Marshal Viscount Wolseley), and in a few seconds the British ensign floated aloft over this massive building; and, although it was shot away again and again, it finally rested there.

Sir Colin Campbell's forces numbered 14,550 men and 32 guns. During the march their losses were 122 killed and 414 wounded. Among the former were 10 officers; among the latter, 35.

Now came the evacuation of the Residency—no small undertaking, with the number of sick, wounded, ladies, children and soldiers' wives, especially as a part of the road leading to the "Dil Khoosha" Palace was under the enemy's fire. I was greatly puzzled how to remove my wife, who was an invalid and unable to walk. The Arab that I had ridden from Seetapore was still in the entrenchment, and as I did not like turning him loose to run the risk of ill-treatment from the rebels, I had made him over to one of the clerks, who promised to look after him and to give him what food he could. On my going in search of him, I found him all right, but in very low condition; however I got some harness and a trap out of the many stored there, and after some difficulty (as he had never seen a collar before in his life) I got him between the shafts of a palkee-gharry, and we began our hazardous journey, the horse behaving as well as could be expected; but our progress was very slow. We were fortunate enough to get across the exposed portion uninjured, and eventually reached the camp prepared for us at the Dil Khoosha, where they gave us a capital supper, which we much enjoyed. We had a very hospitable reception from Major Ouvry and officers (9th Lancers), who were encamped there.

I had to return to the entrenchment to join a small party under Colonel Masters, who was to remain till the last. We left at midnight, moving out quietly, so as to give no intimation to the enemy. Unfortunately Captain Waterman, 13th N. I., one of the party, had fallen asleep from exhaustion, and so got left behind; he did not find out that we had gone till some time after. The shock of finding himself alone had such an effect on his nerves that he had to be sent home in charge of an attendant. The shock can be easily realised by anybody on remembering that this place of terrible memories had formed our garrison during nearly six months, and was now absolutely deserted; and at this hour of midnight not a sound was audible, from what had been a noisy turmoil night and day during this period. I remember vividly to this moment the echo of the footsteps of our small party as we wended our way out of this scene of weird desolation; yet all was activity, with no time for thought, or Waterman would not have met his sad fate. I traversed this road three times that night.

The treasury, consisting of 25 lacs of rupees (£250,000), was all brought out safely by us, having been buried during the siege, and with it a quantity of the ex-king's jewellery; although some had been stolen, a considerable amount remained. We learnt afterwards that the rebels remained in ignorance of our evacuation for many hours after, when they were greatly infuriated, nor did they attempt to enter the garrison till mid-day of the following day. We now received our six months' mail; strange letters they were, many of our friends chiding us for keeping silent, whilst others were painfully anxious as to our safety. The newspapers conveyed to us how great had been the anxiety and sympathy for the Lucknow garrison at home. On my own part I can safely aver that I had a feeling throughout that all would be right, and especially that succour would reach us; the result proved that I was correct.

Sir Colin had given orders that nothing in the form of impedimenta should be taken out of Lucknow; but an amusing story went the round of a large circular drawing-room table, which somebody had evidently a wish to take away, being discovered by the chief, and peremptorily ordered to be abandoned on the road side. Much comment was made on some of the ladies turning out so well dressed, but this arose from their very natural wish to save the best of their wardrobe; this applies to those who had been living in Lucknow.

Sir Colin Campbell informed General Havelock that the honour of a K.C.B. had been conferred upon him; so that he was now "Sir Henry Havelock," to the delight of everybody, whose hero he still remained.

On the 21st, Sir Henry Havelock was attacked by dysentery, and thinking a change of air might do him good he was removed to the Dil Khoosha. On 24th November, but a few days after this honour had been conferred upon him, and to the great grief of all, he died; he had been sinking for two days past, attended to the last by his son. He lived to see the accomplishment of his work: "the rescue of the garrison". Thus died, not only a great general, but a good Christian. His remains were interred in the Alum Bagh.

Events proved that Sir Colin's decision to evacuate the entrenchments at once was the correct one from all points; not a life was sacrificed, all Europeans and natives escaping in safety; also our guns and the whole of the treasury were saved. Nothing but the bare walls were left to the rebels.

Thus, under a most merciful Providence, we had again been relieved—all honour to Sir Colin and his force! who, under heavy losses and enormous difficulties, had bravely mastered all, and preserved our lives, whilst so many had paid the penalty by death. Truly an All-wise Providence had watched over us.

I think we were two days at Dil Khoosha before arrangements were finally completed for the march to Cawnpore, a movement that caused the chief much anxiety, for the enemy were by no means dispersed yet, and to protect a train that extended two miles or so was an arduous task.

At one of our halts a little boy about five years old, son of an officer of the garrison, on loot intent, spotted a fowl that I had procured with great difficulty; he thereupon seized and bolted with it. At this moment I caught sight of him legging it off for all he knew, with the neck of the bird clutched in his tiny hand, the legs dragging along the ground. I gave chase and recovered it. Poor little Tommy wanted it for his mother. On this march I had an experience that seldom falls to one's lot. One of the bearers of the dhooly in which my wife was carried became ill, and the others declared that they were unable to proceed unless he was replaced; I thereupon became a dhooly-bearer myself. The work did not appeal to me, and my shoulders pained me greatly for some time after, being unaccustomed to this work.

We reached Cawnpore without interference, but found we were not out of the wood yet. Cawnpore was attacked by the Gwalior rebels, and the bridge of boats was under fire. However we crossed all right, and got shelter in the entrenchment on the right bank of the river. I can recall the kindness here shown to us by two officers whose names I cannot recall; they gave up their tent and put themselves to great inconvenience to make us comfortable.

From here we were sent off the next day by rail to Allahabad, where we found tents pitched for us in the Fort and everything provided comfortably. Rations were brought in every morning sufficient for the whole number, and this we had to portion off to the different tents according to the number that occupied them. One morning Germon and I were cutting up some meat when he said: "I think this," holding up a large bone, "will do for No. 6 tent; Apthorp who is there is on the sick list, and this will make him good soup". Suddenly a voice from behind: "Please remember, Captain Germon, that there is Mrs. Apthorp in that tent too". This was Mrs. Apthorp herself, very indignant that she was to be put off with a bone. From Allahabad we went to Calcutta by water, under circumstances very different from those of my trip up in 1846. Christmas Day we spent with Mr. and Mrs. Hamilton, my fellow-passengers in the *Queen;* he was opium agent for the Government at Benares.

Among those with us I must not forget to mention my old friend Mrs. Halford; but no "Irish Quadrilles" were asked for this time: the colonel had died during the siege.

At Calcutta we had a great reception: crimson cloth was laid down at the landing-place, the vessels were dressed out in flags, and all were in full dress and very swell for the reception of as ragged-looking a lot of beings as one could well conceive. If I had had the red cloth I was walking on, I thought, some time back I would have made something out of it and not walked on it. The governor-general's carriages were waiting for us, and off we drove to a house that had been taken for us in Chowringhee, where servants and all were provided for us.

Lady Canning came next day, and had an interview with the ladies, asking if anything more could be done for them, and was most kind.

It was arranged for many of the ladies, refugees from the Lucknow Garrison, to sail for home by the SS. *Ava*, a P. and O. vessel, just then leaving. With this number my wife went, taking with her a copious diary of her own and sketches of mine. This ship was wrecked on the coast of Trincomalee; and though passengers and crew were saved by taking to the boats, all was again lost, and of course whilst in Calcutta an outfit had been bought by all. Here again was a calamity. This disaster following upon the terrible months of the Mutiny, to which must be added ill-health, had such an effect on my wife that from the day the *Ava* sailed to the day I left India, 6th September, 1876, she never returned.

A doctor who had been in Lucknow recommended me to have a trip home; so, obtaining fifteen months' leave, I left Calcutta by one of the P. and O. Line, and arrived in England in March 1858. On going down to Great Yarmouth, where my father and mother were living, I had a singular greeting from a large grey parrot belonging to my brother. I had never seen the bird before, but directly I entered the room it called out, "What, my old friend?"

On the voyage back to India, we had a very crowded ship, and among the passengers were thirteen young ladies, all engaged to be married on their arrival in Calcutta. It was amusing to watch them, when the steamer came to an anchor, waiting for their *fiancés*; some had not met for a long time, and hardly knew each other. In two days they were all married. It was on this voyage we had to wait several days at Cairo, as the boat on the other side was late in arriving at Suez. It was in the days when the desert was crossed by rail. Fearing that the train would be very crowded when the time came for leaving, some of us planned to steal a march on the others, and, without saying a word, get away to Suez beforehand. It was most ludicrous: when we got to the station we found the others had planned just the same thing, and were quietly waiting on the platform for the train.

One of the passengers was Colonel Masters, of Lucknow memory, returning to India. He had under his charge a young lady, going to join her father. She was the torment of his life: wherever we stopped she insisted on being taken on shore, sight-seeing; at Malta she would go to the opera, kept the old man up all night, and tired him out completely. What fun we used to have while staying at Shepherd's Hotel! hiring the donkeys, and galloping through the town. I have often thought of that story, told of a sedate old Mohammedan, who, whilst sitting at his stall, saw a lot of griffs careering through the town, and exclaimed: "There are devils and devils, but there is no devil like a Frank in a round hat!"

One has to be up to the way in which the harness is put on these donkeys, or else in turning a corner over one goes. The stirrup leathers are not fastened to the side of the saddle, as ours are, but one long strap goes over the saddle underneath the seat, so if you lean one side more than the other, one foot goes down and the other up in the air, and off you come. There was some fun, too, to be had in the old days when crossing the desert by horse van. Four horses were attached to each, as wild as could be, and under little or no control. It was difficult to start them, but when they did go, it was full gallop over stones or whatever came in the way. The Arabs would persist in driving them without crossing the leader's reins. They went independently to each horse, so there was nothing to prevent them turning round if they liked. On one occasion they did like, came right round abreast of the van, and then kicked the bottom in. They changed at every ten miles, and a supper was provided for us at the expense of the Viceroy of Egypt. How those who were invalids stood the jolting, I don't know. It must have been very trying to them.

CHAPTER X.

CHINA, 1860-1861.

China in preference to Barrickpore—Work in plenty—Drawbacks of the "irregular" system—The unfamiliar hammock—Visit of Sir Robert Napier—Luxurious voyaging—Hostile Chinamen on the Cochin coast—Singapore—A thank-offering—Drastic measures for drunkenness—The "ripples"—At Kowloon—My friend the compradore—Ordered to Shanghai—A panic-stricken official—Barbarities inflicted on Taipings—An annoying incident—A case of conflicting ancestral strains—From the Stone Bridge to the Ningpo Joss House—Polyglot conversation—A deal in watches—Chinese characteristics—Perilous boating—Pleasant relations with the Legation—Back to India—Penang.

On returning to India in November, 1859, I was ordered to Barrickpore to take charge of a section of British soldiers waiting there for an opportunity to be sent home. There was great confusion as to their pay and accounts; it was altogether work that I did not care for; so to get quit of it I sent in my name as volunteer for service in China, a force being fitted out to proceed there. In March, 1860, I received notice that my services were accepted, and was ordered to proceed to Calcutta and join the 15th "Loodhianah Sikhs". On reporting myself to the commanding officer I found him in his tent, which was pitched on the Maidan, very busy with magazine returns, no one to help him. The second in command was on the sick-list and living with friends in Chowringhee, and his adjutant had just come from a British regiment, and as yet was not well up in the routine among natives. The commanding officer welcomed me gladly, gave over to me the books and charge of four companies, and also appointed me quartermaster, so that my work was cut out for me. The regiment was one of those on the irregular system, having only three European officers and a doctor; but now that it was going on service eight more were to be appointed, one for each company. Who was responsible for this arrangement I don't know, but a worse one there could not be. It was a slight on the native officers who had hitherto commanded their companies on parade, which duty they were deprived of when the regiment was ordered on service. Then, again, these officers who were appointed were quite unacquainted with the men, and the men with them; and all knew that it was merely a temporary arrangement, and that when we returned the old system would be renewed. I know the native officers felt it.

The *Winifred* (full rigged ship, 1,150 tons, Captain Rees), was chartered for the conveyance of the head-quarters and right wing, and the *Foujdahar* for the left wing, and on the 15th of March we embarked. Such confusion in getting on board I never saw; hammocks were served out for the men's use, and these had to be slung. Of course the men could give me little or no help, for they had never seen such things before, and they would hardly believe me when I told them they were to sleep in. After slinging one, I told a Sikh to get in and try it; he did try it—went up one side and came out on the other, falling on the deck with such a thud I thought he had broken his back. I gave it up after this, and instead of slinging them, laid the hammocks, side by side, flat on the decks on which the men slept. In the midst of this confusion, who should come on board but Sir Robert Napier, commanding our division, not best pleased at what he saw; but in a short time we got things ship-shape and settled for the night.

Next morning, the 16th, we dropped down the river in tow of H.M.S. *Magicienne* (Captain Commerell, V.C.), a most luxurious way of performing a sea voyage: no vibration of the engine, no sails to tend, and an even keel—nothing can be more delightful.

Off the Cochin China coast we had a little excitement. Requiring sand for cleaning our decks, the *Magicienne* took us into a small bay, anchored, and sent a boat ashore. As we also were anxious to go, Captain Rees launched a boat for us, and off we went; but we had not been there long before we heard a great noise of gongs, and looking round saw a body of Chinamen coming down from a fort that overlooked the bay, and when they came a little nearer, beginning to fire in our direction. Not being prepared for a fight, we got into our boat again and shoved off, but Captain Commerell was not going to let them have it all their own way. He got the *Magicienne* into position, so that her guns could bear, and then sent a few round shot through the walls of their fort; out they bolted, and we saw no more of them. In addition to their muskets each man carried a large flag.

Singapore was our first port, and here we stayed a few days. The day of our arrival a number of boats with fruit, fish, etc., came alongside, and as I was on the companion ladder buying some pine apples a native officer asked me if any of the fish were alive; if so, he and his brother officers wished me to buy one for them, and then let it go overboard as a kind of thank-offering for having performed thus far of their journey in safety. Out of those I showed them they selected an ugly-looking specimen, and asked me to throw it back into the sea; on inquiring of the Chinaman the price, he said 6d. This the native officers would not hear of, and they handed me 20 rupees (£2), which I was to give the man. When I did so his astonishment was most ludicrous; he gave a yell which brought his wife who was with him to his side, and, after he had told her, they both seized their oars and made for shore, afraid, I suppose, that we might repent of our bargain.

We made rather a brave show here, as there were a number of French vessels also on their way to China with troops; the native officers were much interested when I told them where they had come from, asked me questions about the distance, etc., and said it was capital "bundobust" (management) to arrive as we did together. One day two Sikhs who had been on shore on leave got drunk, and when the boat in which they were came alongside they were so helpless that a rope had to be let down from the yard-arm to hoist them on board. The commanding officer was so indignant that when they were half-way up he ordered the rope to be slackened and a dip in the sea to be given them; this was done, but when it came to hauling them up again the rope fouled, and one could not for a long time either haul them on board or lower them into the boat again, and there they swung helpless in mid-air. Those on board the French vessels thought, I believe, that we were hanging the men.

While lying becalmed in the Straits of Malacca we witnessed that curious phenomenon of the sea called the "ripples". There was not a breath of air at the time, but suddenly a dark line was seen on the horizon, gradually giving every indication of a fresh breeze coming. Nearer and nearer it came, and yet no wind. The sea was broken up into small waves, which beat against the side of the vessel, and then went on beyond, leaving the sea as smooth as before. This was repeated several times. I could gain no information as to the cause, but it was very wonderful.

After forty-five years I cannot remember all the dates of different occurrences, but it was not many days after this that we cast anchor off Hong-Kong. Our orders were to go into camp at Kowloon, on the opposite side of the bay, and I was sent on shore with the tents to see the camp pitched. Whilst superintending this, my mind was greatly exercised about dinner for those who would shortly arrive. I had taken charge of the mess, but there was nothing to be got where I was, and our servants had not come. Presently a Chinaman came up to me and said he was a compradore, and asked if we wanted dinner; I said that was exactly what I did want; he said, "How many?" I told him. "Can do," was his reply, and off he went. By the time the others arrived they were cheered by the sight of an excellent dinner laid out: roast chickens, roast ducks, sweets, with beer, brandy and soda-water. I engaged my friend, the compradore, as mess-man for as long as we remained at Kowloon, and a capital one he was.

When the time came for us to move up north, we were greatly disappointed on hearing we were to go to Shanghai and protect the settlement from the Taipings who threatened it. We had all looked forward to going to Pekin. On arrival at Shanghai I was sent in command of two companies to occupy a joss house at the stone bridge across the Soochow Creek. Here I was joined by a party of marines under a major, and also some French troops. And off we went six miles into the country to keep back the Taipings, who were reported as advancing on the settlement; but we saw nothing of them, so came back again. It was a very disagreeable march, as it poured with rain the whole time; I started wearing a full suit of waterproof, but returned minus the whole; the heat and the weight of the garments were unbearable, so I had cast them adrift one by one.

It was ludicrous, the state of panic that was inspired by these Taipings amongst the Chinese authorities in the town. The taotai (governor) was so alarmed that one day he ordered the bearers of his sedan chair to take him to the quarters of a marine officer who had a post on the city wall, and there he insisted on remaining until he thought it safe to go back to his yamen, which was not for several days. When he did get a chance he behaved with abominable cruelty. On one occasion a Taiping commander was captured and put in prison. Every morning one of his nails was drawn out, first from his fingers, then from his toes; after this he was decapitated. I watched a regiment going out to meet these rebels. If beating of gongs and a great display of flags had anything to do with it, they ought to have annihilated any force brought against them. First, they were marched to one of the gateways, where six wretched prisoners were brought out and their heads taken off by the executioners; then the flags were dipped in the blood to bring them luck, I was told, and to make them invincible. It did not answer. In the afternoon they returned a very sorry lot, what there were of them, for they had fallen into an ambush and half their number were killed. After what I had seen, I must say I was not sorry for them. We had a very quiet time of it at the Stone Bridge Joss House; our position was never threatened at all. News from the north was what we were all looking out for, but one day I thought we were in for a little brush with the rebels. I had gone into the settlement after breakfast, and on my return found no one at the Joss House but the quarter guard. On asking where the regiment was, I was told the commanding officer had taken them out a short distance, as he heard the enemy's cavalry had approached somewhat near. After a walk of about four miles I found them all in a small village, doing nothing but watching a body of the enemy not more than 200 yards off. The commanding officer would do nothing—would not let us stir from the village; and what he went out for, I don't know. After an hour or so, we were marched back again. I was so annoyed at our having made such an exhibition of ourselves, that I asked the commanding officer why he came at all. He said: "Well, Ruggles, my father was an Irishman and my mother was a Quakeress. Sometimes I'm all for fighting, and then again all for peace; I can't make up my mind." Nothing will show better than this what an extraordinary character he was.

After being at the Stone Bridge for about six

weeks we were ordered to the Ningpo Joss House, where the left wing was already quartered. This was not so pleasant as that we had vacated, as it was close to the city walls and more confined.

I wonder how it is that men of different nations when they meet manage to make themselves understood. I passed one day a Sikh, a French soldier, and a Marine, discussing the value of some loot the Frenchman had got hold of; it was a queer jumble that they talked, but they managed somehow to express their meaning.

The French left at Shanghai were very envious at what their comrades brought down from the north. Amongst other things were a number of gold watches set with pearls at the back, etc., and these they sold for large prices to the merchants in the settlements. A bright idea struck one of those left behind. He went to a watchmaker, and bought up a number of small watches made in Geneva and ornamented in the same way but not with genuine stones; and these he took round and disposed of for handsome sums, as curios from the Summer Palace, Pekin.

I don't think there can be in the world a more unfeeling race than the Chinese. On one occasion some villages about two or three miles out were burnt to the ground by the Taipings, and the inhabitants fled for refuge into Shanghai. Not much sympathy did they get: the inhabitants would have none of them, and, although the weather was cold and wet, allowed them to remain outside and manage as best they could. There were a number of women and children, some of them sick, who must have suffered terribly. I believe it is looked upon as unlucky to give shelter to a sick person.

I often thought, while in China, what a curious state of affairs it was: up in the north we were fighting the Imperialists, and in the south we were taking their part and fighting the rebels for them; but everything is topsy-turvey in China. I never liked the Chinese: they are cruel and treacherous. While at Kowloon I often had to go across the bay to Hong-Kong, about three miles, and to do so had to charter one of the boats that plied to and fro. Now these boats were not built after the Chinese pattern, but were ships' long boats carrying a large latteen sail; there was no ballast, and to make them still more crank planks were laid across the seats, forming a deck, leaving a small cockpit in the stern to steer from. On this deck the boatman, his wife and children all squatted. Several times we were nearly capsized, but they never cared: the children all had empty gourds fastened round their necks, so that if they did go overboard they were perfectly safe; I have seen them bobbing about in the water quite unconcerned. One thing I was warned about, either to steer myself or keep a watch on the man who was steering, instances having been known of a passenger being either knocked on the head or stabbed, and his body thrown overboard.

The troops were now (May, 1861) being ordered back to India, matters having been settled at Pekin; and accordingly on the 21st of that month we got orders to embark on board H.M.S. *Urgent*, Captain Hire. We had made several friends among the members of the British Legation during our stay at Shanghai, and had been most hospitably entertained by them on several occasions. From the first they gave us all the aid they could in dealing with the Chinese. The night before we started they came on board to wish us *bon voyage*.

I don't think any of us were sorry to leave; I was glad myself to get back to India, as I liked neither the country nor the people. Probably our short stay did not enable us to know them well enough, but what I did know of them was not favourable. Perhaps this may have been my fault, as I have heard different opinions from those who had a lengthened stay.

Our voyage back was not eventful. We put in at the island of Penang; and, as we were to stay the day, took the opportunity to give the men a run on shore; we made a big picnic of it and they thoroughly enjoyed it. The scenery is very beautiful. Getting hold of a guide we marched the men to a celebrated waterfall, and above this on the banks of the stream made our bivouac. How the men revelled in a bath!

CHAPTER XI.

INDIA AGAIN.

Arrival at Calcutta—Inspections—Interview with the chief—Ordered to Lucknow—A nocturnal party in strange attire—The tinned sausages—Ordered to Seetapore—Sad memories—Appointed second in command of 19th Punjabees—A night alarm—Mishap with the mess plates—Troops at Morar—Gwalior fort—A mess bungalow secured—Court-martial on a European—Capping stories—Incredulous listeners—An unfortunate addition to the rice—" Kuch Nes"—Tall peas—Sport with Stafford at Mahona—A sensitive spaniel.

THE month of June saw us back in India again, and on arriving at Calcutta we received orders to proceed to Raneegunge by rail. The commander-in-chief, Sir Hugh Rose, came to the station to look at us. I am afraid we did not look very smart; for our consolation, he said he would send General Showers in a few days to inspect us. This he did about a week after, and I am glad to say that all went off satisfactorily. As the regiment would revert now to its former complement of three European officers, the services of those who had been with it in China were no longer required, although we remained with it for the present; and what to do was the question. I determined at last to go to Calcutta and see the chief. One day in the week (Wednesday) any one by applying to the A.D.C. could see him. After hearing all I had to say, he asked what it was that I wanted. I said: "The second in command of a regiment". He then wanted to know if I had ever served in a British regiment, and on my replying "No," he said: "I think it a good thing for officers in your service to know something of the routine that can be learnt there". Of course I said I would go if he wished.

Shortly after this, the regiment was ordered to Lucknow by bullock train—I taking charge of four companies, the men distributed in waggons—journeying about forty miles a day. At one of the rest houses where I halted an amusing incident occurred. Instead of sleeping in my cart, as I generally did, I moved into the bungalow, and in the middle of the night the old Khansamah woke me up, and said that a carriage had arrived with a gentleman and two ladies, and they wanted a room. Of course I prepared to turn out and go to my cart again, but before I could get out of the way in they came: two ladies, one old and one young, and a gentleman; the former in their night attire, the old lady wearing a huge nightcap. I also was in my sleeping suit. A funny party we looked! But as they did not seem to mind, and wanted some supper, we all sat down and had a meal together; and this in the middle of the night!

At another of the rest houses, I had given out to the Khansamah for my breakfast a tin of Oxford sausages; but as they did not turn out very good, when they came to table, I told him to throw them away. Do you think that he threw them away? Not he! The old ruffian cooked them up into a savoury dish, and served them for breakfast to the subaltern who came after me, charging him three rupees eight annas (7s.).

In a few days I was in orders to join the 34th Foot Border Regiment at Seetapore. It was a strange coincidence my being ordered back to these two old stations, Lucknow and Seetapore. At the latter station I had to buy a house, as there were none to be rented; but it was not expensive: 500 rupees, I think, I paid for it.

Almost the first thing I did was to go and see the ruins of our old cantonment. It was a sad sight: a heap of ruins marked the spot where our bungalow had stood, all having been destroyed by the mutineers. I tried to find out if there were any of our books or pictures at the native shops in the town, but without success. Probably, if they were there, those who had them would have been afraid to own it.

I had joined the 34th, December 24th, 1861, and after the report of the inspection had gone in, in the following year, the chief, Sir Hugh Rose, was good enough to remember me: through the military secretary I received intimation that I had been appointed second in command of the 19th Punjabees stationed at Meerut. I joined on June 22nd, 1862. The regiment was commanded by Major Stafford, who had raised it in 1858, and a very fine regiment it was. Towards the end of the year we were ordered to Gwalior—on the way forming an escort to the commander-in-chief, who was on a tour. An event occurred on the march down which threatened at one time to turn out most disastrously for us. One night the camp was disturbed by a most terrific scream from the direction of the tents where the staff were. It turned out that a thief had got into Major Gawler's tent, and the Major, trying to seize him, was stabbed between the ribs. The man was a Pathan, and when I saw him I really thought, and so did Stafford, that he was one of our own men. Eventually to our great relief this turned out not to be the case. He was a man hired for the march by Major Gawler's servant. Sir Hugh was very angry at first, and called for a sketch showing how our sentries were posted. I made one for him, and he acknowledged that it was not our fault.

In crossing the Chumba River the hackery (cart) carrying our mess plates, etc., overbalanced and went into the river. The chief on hearing this, and knowing that our dinner would be greatly delayed in consequence, sent his A.D.C. to invite us all to dine with him. The cart and its contents were afterwards recovered.

We reached Morar, Gwalior, in December, and for some time remained in tents, no houses being vacant; but as it was the cold weather it did not much matter. With us at Morar was H.M. 81st.,

Renny's Troop of Horse Artillery, the Elephant Battery, 1st N.I. and Murray's Jat Horse (14th Lancers).

The country surrounding the cantonments was not attractive: a bare plain with nothing to relieve the eye except the fort at Gwalior, about three miles distant, situated on a rocky eminence in shape resembling a huge ironclad. Inside in a deep hollow were cut out of the rock figures of Hindoo idols. It had been in our possession, I believe, since 1842, and the maharajah was making every effort to have it given up to him again.

In the early part of 1863 we managed to rent a bungalow for the mess, a large house having two suites of rooms, besides anteroom and dining-room. As the two latter were sufficient for our small mess, Stafford and I occupied the others.

On December 20th I had to attend a court-martial as interpreter. A European was tried for getting drunk and killing a donkey; he was found on the road fast asleep with the donkey for a pillow.

India is a great place for stories, true and otherwise. They have been told over and over again, but I don't think they ever cease to amuse, and there may be some who have never heard them :—

Years ago there were a colonel and a major, who were both renowned for drawing the long bow, and to whom it was a great amusement to listen, but chiefly so when they could be got together, as it was considered incumbent on each to cap any story which the other had told. On one occasion they were both dining out at the same mess, and one of them was asked, by way of starting him, what was the most wonderful thing he had seen in the East. "Well," he said, "that is rather a difficult question to answer; I have seen so many; but I can tell you what I saw on one occasion when I was returning from furlough, which I thought very strange. Off the Cape the look-out hailed the deck, and said he saw something ahead; he could not make out what, but it looked like a raft, and seated on it was a man flourishing a paddle. They bore down to have a look, and when close were surprised to see a man astride a hen-coop, working a paddle and smoking a big cheroot. The captain hailed him, and asked what on earth he was doing, and did he want any help? 'No,' said the other, 'I am going home. I have beer inside, but I should feel obliged for a box of matches, as I have used all I had.' The matches were given him, and he proceeded on his way, and I have never seen him since."

Well, they had a glass of sherry all round after hearing this, just to wash it down; and then the other story-teller was watched to hear what he had to tell. The rejoinder was very clever. He rose from his seat, walked round the table to where the other was sitting, clapped him on the shoulder, and said: "My dear fellow, I am delighted to meet you. I have looked for you everywhere. I can quite corroborate your story in every particular, for *I was the man on that raft*," and throwing a matchbox on the table, added: "That's the *empty matchbox the captain gave me*".

Another: Two men while at home on furlough met at a dinner; and during the evening a lady asked one of them the same question as I have related above, namely, what struck him as the most curious thing he had seen in India—what impressed him most after his first arrival. He said there was so much that was new and strange that he hardly knew, but he recollected being greatly struck with the way in which the elephant stretched out his trunk to allow the mahout to walk up and get to his seat on the animal's neck; but this they would not believe—"could not," they said. He appealed to his friend to back him up, but he only shook his head, and would have nothing to say to it. When outside he was taken to task: "Why didn't you corroborate what I said?" "My dear fellow," he replied, "it would not have been the slightest use; I could see they would not believe what you were saying on any account, and they would only have put us *both* down as liars instead of one." Of course what he described can be seen often enough where there are any elephants.

Numerous are the stories of the amusing mistakes made by new arrivals in India. I made one myself, even before I landed. As the *Queen* proceeded up the Hoogly, a boat came off with letters for the captain. After delivering these the boat was towed up. I, looking over the stern, saw the crew at dinner; they were seated round a large dish of rice, and, thinking to add something to their very plain food, I went below and brought up some biscuits, one of which I threw down to them. It fell into the dish, when, to my astonishment, they pitched all the rice overboard, climbed on deck, and made a formal complaint that I had spoilt their dinner, as their caste prevented them from touching it after it had been defiled by my biscuit falling into it. I had to compensate them for the loss of their dinner!

The following is called the story of the "Kuch Nes". A griff going out shooting, attracted, as he said, by the beautiful birds he saw, shot everything that he came across, and brought back a coolie load in triumph. His bearer, who had been in the service of a man who had shot all kinds of game, on looking them over, put them aside, one by one, saying as he did so, "Kuch Ne, Kuch Ne" (nothing, nothing), meaning that none of them were game birds or worth anything. On going to mess that night he was asked what sport he had had, and he said he had got a good bag of "Kuch Nes".

And yet another: A discussion was going on between two who were boasting of what their gardens could produce. One was great on peas, and told how much better they were than others'. His companion said that last year he got out some seed from England, and he continued, "You may imagine the height my peas grew, when I tell you that an elephant was found among them that had been missing for a fortnight!"

On the 23rd, Stafford and I drove to Mahona, on the road leading to Bombay, he for shooting, and I for fishing; and we put up at the Dak Bungalow, situated on the banks of a large river. During the five days we were there Stafford had tolerable luck, considering how wild the game was, but I had a very small bag, only two mahseer, small (about eight or ten lb. each), but they were nice clean fish. The following was Stafford's bag: 9 ravine deer, 9 black buck, 5 bustard, 5 pea fowl, 2½ couple of ducks, 6 brace of rock pigeon, 2 Niel Ghye, 4 hares, 14 brace of partridges. We returned to Morar on the 29th.

On those mornings when there was no párade I generally met Colonel Wright, the magistrate, accompanied by his dog, a handsome clumber spaniel, named "Carlo". This dog was invariably attacked by a number of pariahs, which rushed out of a village as he passed. This so irritated Wright, that one day he took his gun with him, and when the dogs came out he shot the leading one. Carlo went up to it, sniffed at it, looked his master in the face, and then bolted off home as hard as he could go. When Wright reached home Mrs. Wright said: "What have you done to Carlo? He came back a little while ago, and has gone under the bed to hide and will not come out." From that day he would never go out with his master again.

CHAPTER XII.

BHOOTAN.

Agra and Allyghur—Lucky escapes—Trains in collision—Mr. Barnes at Colgong—Recalcitrant baggage animals—Karajambus—Major Stafford unwell—My little brigade—Cold night work—Harrassed by arrows—Rushing the stockade—The enemy's flag—Commendation from superiors—Leeches—Sad end of the goat—A disastrous march—Agility of cholera patients—Death of Lieutenant Kennedy—Trying climate—At Julpesh—Bamboo houses—Inspection by General Tyler—Stafford re-joins—W—— of "ours"—Renewed operations against the Bhooteahs—Strange use for a telegraph wire—A cork bed and a cork mattress—Monkeys and dogs—Destructive vengeance—Freak of an absentee caterer—Sagacity of an elephant.

We were not quite a year at Morar. In 1864 we were ordered to Agra, *en route* to Allyghur, our future station. At Agra we remained in tents for three or four months, and then went on to Allyghur.

The country all round Agra and Allyghur was excellent for sport; black buck were plentiful. In riding after a wounded one on one occasion, Subadar Ahmudzai, a Pathan native officer, went down a blind well, horse, dog and all, and, strange to say, none of them were hurt. An accident similar to this happened at Cawnpore during the Mutiny: a cavalry regiment was charging over a sandy plain, and one of the troopers went down a well, and in this instance also I believe neither man nor horse was hurt.

Early in 1865 we received orders to proceed at once on service to Bhootan. We left by special train on the 17th of February for Allahabad, and on the way got knocked about by a train than ran into us from behind. I got a blow on the head which made me feel very stupid; Stafford was knocked off his seat, and doubled up on the floor amidst broken seraies, etc.; but Copland, our adjutant, was the worst off, as he received a severe cut on the head. We arrived at Allahabad about 4 P.M.

Continuing our journey next day, we reached Colgong on the 21st, and were very hospitably received and entertained by Mr. Barnes, an indigo planter, at whose house we remained all day. Next morning, at 5.30 A.M., we left for Karagola Ghat, on the opposite side, Mr. Barnes very kindly placing his own boat at the disposal of the officers, and putting on board ample supply of refreshments. It took us five hours to cross.

From here we went on by double marches, in vile weather all the way—nothing but rain in torrents; besides this the carriage was bad. The bullocks that were provided for us gave infinite trouble; not surprising, considering they were unaccustomed to this work. They continually pitched their loads, and went off into the jungle. The worst of it was, the sepoys could give little help, for the bullocks had never seen one before and shied off at once if the men attempted to adjust their burdens. The elephants also were very unsteady; one morning whilst watching the loading I saw one, which had just had his load adjusted, suddenly raise his trunk, and give a scream, and charge another which was some distance off.

On the 14th of March we reached a place called Karajambus, on the right bank of the Toorsa, and only five miles from the general's head-quarters camp. Here we were joined by the head-quarters, 18th N. I., under Captain Winson. Soon after our arrival the general sent for Major Stafford, and a few hours after he was gone I was sent for. The general told me that Major Stafford was too unwell for the work he proposed he should carry out, and therefore I was to have the command of the column in to-morrow's operations. The plan was, that while the force in the general's camp was to make a feint attack on the stockades in front, I was to go to the left over the hills, and, crossing the river, attack them on their right. My little brigade consisted of the 19th P. N. I., 18th N. I., two guns, two howitzers and forty sappers under Captain Perkins, R.E.; the guns and howitzers being on elephants. I was to start that same evening, as the march would be a long one, and somewhat difficult, for we should have to penetrate a dense jungle, and crossing the river might take time, as it was a roaring torrent and we should have to wade. I got back as quickly as possible to camp, and made my arrangements, and by

7 P.M. we started. What a march it was! Up to about midnight a steep climb through dense jungle, so dark that we had almost to feel our way. At 12 we halted at a small village, Suntabarree, and there had a rest for about an hour, and got some refreshment. Then on again—this time down-hill until we came to one of the branches of the Toorsa. When clear of the jungle we had some light from the waning moon. A cold wind blew down the gorge, making it very unpleasant to plunge into the stream which we had to ford. The bed consisted of huge boulders; this and the rapid stream made one's footing very precarious, not to speak of the depth of the water, which was a little above one's waist. I nearly came to utter grief. Half-way across I slipped on one of the rocks, went a header into the water, and was being carried along at a great pace when one of my orderlies reached out his rifle, which I got hold of, and so managed to reach the bank. One more stream we had to cross, not so difficult, though deeper; but how cold it was! We now found ourselves at the foot of the spur of the hills on which the stockades were, but confronted by a high bank about forty or fifty feet high. Up this it was impossible to get the elephants with the guns, etc.; so we had to leave them behind with a company as guard, and pushed on ourselves. It was fatiguing work, up one hill and down another, till at last, at 11 A.M. on the morning of the 15th, we came to a part that looked down on the stockade. A

feeble fire was opened upon us, as we came in view; but as soon as they saw us advance at the double they bolted and took refuge in the stockade at the top of the hill and directly facing us. As we had no guns, there was no alternative but to make an assault, and try to escalade it. While waiting for more men to come up we were exposed to a fire from muskets and bows and arrows, which did not do much harm; but I must say that arrows try one more than bullets: you see the former, but not the latter. As soon as I thought we had enough men, we moved on, and when near enough rushed up to the walls. These were about twenty feet high, built of loose rough stones, held in their places by beams of wood at intervals of three or four feet. We soon managed to get over, and then the affair was at an end. Those in the third stockade, to our right and lower down, when they saw that the others had fallen, bolted.

Our casualties were very small; only a few had trifling wounds. We remained on the hill all day and all that night. How cold it was! After this the force was broken up; but we were left for the present to occupy the stockades, to prevent any return of the Bhooteahs.

I still have the flag which they flew in the stockade; it is made of crimson China silk, about seven feet long in the hoist and a foot and a half broad, with three small dark blue pennants in the fly, denoting the rank of the commandant.

The following telegram was received from Sir

Hugh Rose, commander-in-chief: "Thank your troops, especially the 19th under Captain Ruggles, for the good and gallant service they have done. Ask him if there is anything I can do for him." Also a letter from the military secretary ran as follows: "Tell Captain Ruggles that the chief would give him the command of a regiment but his rank prevents it. Ask him if there is any other way of serving him." At the time of my writing this (1906), this State, Bhootan, has come to the fore owing to its importance as forming a stepping-stone into Thibet.

I managed to get two good mahseer out of the Toorsa, and very welcome they were, as supplies were scarce; there was no game to be had, although the country looked so promising. We were most terribly troubled with leeches, neither gaiters nor long boots being any protection; the bushes were full of them, to my surprise, as I always thought they abode in ponds. I remember one morning when Bergman, who slept in my tent, awoke, he found his pillow covered with blood: the leeches had got up inside the roof and dropped down during the night.

We had had a goat sent up to us, secured from one of the villages with some difficulty, to supply us with milk, and great care was taken of this animal. One night we heard it making a most distressing sound; we got up but could only see that the poor beast was in great pain; the next morning it was dead, and good-bye to milk for our tea. Then the cause was discovered. Baldwin, who was a great naturalist, had a jar of arsenical soap to cure the skin of birds that he wished to preserve. His servant had left this about open and the poor goat, I suppose, thinking it looked good, had eaten some of it.

In June we were ordered to Julpesh, where the 5th Cavalry under Major Gough, V.C., had already gone. Our last march was very disastrous. In the first place the heat was very great and the guide misled us: instead of a twelve-mile march it turned out twenty-five. Then cholera broke out and we soon had a number of patients who had to be carried in bullock carts. At one part the "track" (for one could call it nothing else) led between two rice fields. Elephants carrying tents, etc., led the way; then came the carts with the sick. Presently there was a stoppage, and on going to ascertain the cause I found that the elephant which was carrying two large boxes of hospital stores had turned vicious and barred the way; he then gave himself a shake, and off came the boxes; these he trampled under foot till pills and draughts were in a pulp. He then turned round to see what he could do next. The carts with the sick seemed to attract him, and he made a stride towards them. The bullocks seeing him coming threw off their yokes and bolted, and the men who were on the carts, *supposed to be so very ill*, jumped off and followed their example. The elephant raised his forefoot and plumped it down on the cart, making it as flat as a pancake. This seemed to satisfy him and he became quiet; all the same he would not allow the mahout to go near him, but permitted a small boy, the son of the mahout, to place a chain round his legs. The doctor was much concerned regarding his cholera patients, as he thought this stampede would cause the death of half of them; but instead of that he found them sitting under a tree as lively as crickets.

Lieutenant Kennedy, who had joined us, died on the march from cholera. The heat was excessive, sultry and oppressive to a degree, as rain fell during the night, and a very hot sun succeeded in the morning; and added to this a perfect stillness in the air made it almost unbearable. Our sepoys, who mostly came from the north, could hardly stand it, and with the greatest difficulty completed the march.

At Julpesh we had temporary houses made entirely of bamboo, raised five feet from the ground; not at all uncomfortable, but the floor of the rooms swayed somewhat when one moved about. General Tyler came and inspected us; all went off well. Major Stafford, who had gone to the hills on medical certificate on the 18th of March, rejoined in October.

The doings of W—— of "ours" amused us much: he had ways of his own in ordinary transactions different from any one's, and at times they were very funny. For instance, he would send to Calcutta to a firm with whom he had dealings a signed cheque, leaving the amount to be filled in by them. He *would* have it this was the correct way! On returning from leave, which he had spent in England, he told us with great glee that one day, being in London, and not knowing where to go for luncheon, he asked a policeman, who directed him, and when he arrived at the place he found all the knives and forks chained to the table! At Julpesh we used to amuse ourselves by throwing a round shot. W——, in order to try if he could beat the best throw, would practise half through the night by himself, and on one occasion nearly managed to injure himself severely by trying to carry this shot whilst swimming across a small stream that ran close by.

In the month of October orders came for us to go to Buxa, where another expedition was being got ready against the Bhooteahs. From there we marched into the hills, and came to a halt at a place called Tabzee, and then commenced making a road towards the capital, Punakha; but when we had made it as far as Meercham, about ten miles, work was stopped, as the Bhooteahs had given in. At times the weather at Tabzee was unpleasant to a degree, cold and miserably wet.

I was amused one day at hearing a conversation between two sepoys regarding the telegraph wire that was being laid. The end had been buried in the ground close to the spring where we obtained our water. One wanted to know why it was taken there; the other said: "Why, of course, to let the Sahib Logue know if the water is good or not".

A comical mistake was made by M—— while we were in camp. I had a cork bed that I found very serviceable in the damp weather; it folded up very compactly, so that it could be carried in the hand, and took up very little or no room. M—— wished for one like it, and wrote to Calcutta for a cork *mattress.* In due course three coolies came staggering up the hill with a load as big as a house; it was about eight feet long, and four broad. *N.B.* A bed is not a mattress!

There was a large number of monkeys in the forest, and one day a party had rather an unpleasant experience. If there is one thing a monkey hates more than another it is to have a small dog barking and yelping at him. On the occasion referred to some dogs were with the party, and they were walking on a path on one side of which was a deep precipice and on the other a high mountain. Some monkeys appeared above them, and the dogs began barking as usual. The monkeys disappeared for a time, but, going a little farther, the party was assailed by a volley of stones, and had to beat a hasty retreat.

I can remember another case where they avenged themselves on a small dog that annoyed them. It was in a small tope (grove), and the dog, seeing the monkeys in the trees, set up an incessant barking. There were, on one of the lower branches, two old monkeys who bore it for some time, till at last one came quietly down, on the opposite side to where the dog was, slipped round, caught hold of him by the scruff of his neck, and was up the tree again like lightning. Then these two old monkeys cuffed him soundly, and when they thought he had had enough let him drop to the ground.

Once while out sketching in the hills at the back of our camp at Tabzee, I saw a troop of monkeys pass among the tree tops, leaping from branch to branch, and I noticed that all selected the same branch to alight upon as the leader.

Another story of the Bundur Log (monkey people) I may as well relate here; it occurred at Mooltan soon after we occupied the fort. We were then living in some dome-roofed rooms that were built round three sides of the square. Two of them had been knocked into one to form a mess room for the Artillery; in the room adjoining a monkey belonging to one of the officers had been tied up; he was a vicious brute, and his temper was made worse by the mess servants, who teased him as they passed, offering him food and then taking it away. But he had his revenge. He began quietly to undermine the partition wall, taking out the bricks one by one until he had a hole large enough; and then he watched his opportunity. The next time the servants came to lay the table he opened fire, throwing brick after brick as hard and fast as he could straight down the table, smashing the glass and crockery that was on it, and putting the servants to flight. At Tabzee a very eccentric officer, who had charge of the sapper mess, told me with great glee one evening that he had ordered monkey for the dinner. *N.B.* He was dining out himself!

An incident showing how sagacious the elephant is occurred while at Tabzee. A shooting expedition was got up to search the jungle at the foot of the hills, with the possibility of getting a rhinoceros, which the commanding officer succeeded in doing. While the elephants were beating through the high grass, one of the sportsmen, a doctor, in pulling out his handkerchief, pulled with it a fifty rupee note, which fluttered away. Search was made without success, but on their return later in the day one of the elephants suddenly stopped. The mahout spoke to him; he then stretched out his trunk, lifted from the bottom of the grass a piece of paper and gave it to the driver. This turned out to be the fifty rupee note.

CHAPTER XIII.

SIMLA.

Return to Allyghur—To Simla on leave—Trip to Narkhunda—Tragic death of Lady Brind—Bobbery Pack at Allyghur—The fatal lampreys—Nynee Tal—The yellow-back out of place—Native sense of humour—Heavy loads carried by women—A bribe for wild coolies—Miscalling of names—In orders for Peshawur—Memorials to General Nicholson—Tame black buck—Earthquake scare at Attock—Cholera precautions upset by frogs—Cholera deaths—A versatile priest—Fruit trade arrested—Suggestion from comparison of cholera poison and snake-bite poison—Strange cases of recovery—Shere Ali—Interesting document possessed by Bahadur Khan—Instances of native prescience.

WE were not sorry when the order came for the camp to be broken up, and for us to return to our station. We arrived at Allyghur in the early part of 1866.

In May I went to Simla on leave. A very good time I had. Especially did I enjoy a trip out to Narkhunda, forty miles. There is a capital dak bungalow, from which one obtains a magnificent view of a snowy range. On the way I passed the spot where Lady Brind a short while previously met with such a terrible death. She was on her pony sketching, and a pheasant flew out of the jungle; the whirr frightened the pony, and his hind legs dropped over the edge of the precipice; he made a violent effort to recover himself, the syce tried to help him by seizing the reins, but they all three went over and were killed.

I returned to Allyghur in September, when a "Bobbery Pack" was started. Bow-wows of all denominations were enlisted; but, in order to give them a good example to follow, the commanding officer bought a couple of fox-hounds; it was not long, however, before one came to a very untimely end. In a consignment of stores from England for the mess were some tins of lampreys; one day one was opened on trial. No one liked them, and the khitmatgar was told to throw it away. The hound got hold of it, ate the contents and died. How history repeats itself!

In 1867 I went to Nynee Tal on two months' leave; it is a lovely spot, the scenery not so grand as Simla, but I think much prettier. The lake is an advantage that other hill stations are without; water is always a great addition to scenery.

The first Sunday I was there a ludicrous incident happened. A young lady while being carried to church in her jampan had been reading a yellow-covered novel. Before going into church she left this book in the jampan. After she had gone one of her jampanees (carriers), seeing that all had books with them, and not knowing the difference, thought it was left behind by accident; so he took it up, and holding it in both hands, well in front of him, marched boldly into the church, up the aisle, and placed it on the shelf before the owner. Of course the natives saw no humour in it, but to us it was very funny. I have often wondered if they do appreciate a joke. I am rather inclined to think they do sometimes. I recollect on one occasion our regimental baboo being taken to task for not having the lines on a form he had to make out straight. He looked up and said quietly: "Sir, it is a very difficult thing to rule straight lines with a crooked ruler".

It was astonishing what heavy loads the women of these parts were able to carry up and down the hills. They passed through our camp frequently, carrying on their backs large baskets full of turnips, secured by a band of rattan passing across the forehead. On one occasion when they stopped to rest we went to have a look at them. On our trying to lift one of these baskets, not a man in the camp could raise it off the ground.

The baggage master had great trouble with the coolies employed to carry our traps. They were wild beings, utterly unaccustomed to any kind of restraint, and continually walked off and turned up again when it suited them. He at last hit upon a plan that answered admirably. He had a small musical box that he had got from Delhi as loot. It was beautifully made, and, I should say, had been sent as a present to the king. When wound up to play, a small trap-door opened on the lid and out hopped a small canary, flapped its wings and sang while the tune played. He showed this to one of the coolies one day, and the man was so delighted with it that he told all the others, and they petitioned to be allowed to see it too; so he arranged a little entertainment for them in the evening when work was done, but excluded all who had given trouble during the day. It worked well: he had no complaint as to their conduct afterwards.

The natives have a funny way of miscalling names, and can seldom or never pronounce English names correctly. The judge at Allyghur had two dogs; one he called "Caliban" and the other "Sycorax"; these the natives changed into "Carrywan" and "Stickowax". At Buxa there was at the post-office a great accumulation of letters which the baboo was most anxious to get rid of, amongst them a large number for a Lieutenant de Bourbel. One morning the general's A.D.C., Captain Beaumont, went for his letters, and when he gave his name, the baboo remarked: "Excuse me, sir, but I think your name must be 'De Bourbel'".

In 1868 we were in orders for Peshawur, a long march, and as it turned out a hot one. We started in August, and to minimise the heat we changed the usual order: instead of starting in the morning we marched late in the afternoon, and found it an advantage. In the Magulla Pass—one march, I think, before reaching the Indus—we passed a monument on a high rock on the left of the road, and on the opposite side, to the right, is a fountain, both of these to the memory of General Nicholson; although it was rather dark at the time, I managed to get a sketch of them.

When at Allyghur we had two tame black buck in the lines; they had been caught when very young, and when once they got accustomed to it all never left the parade ground. When the regiment marched past in review they always went with the band. Before we left one died, poisoned, I believe, and the other we lost on this march to Peshawur. It was tied up every night to one of the poles of the shemianah under which the commanding officer used to sleep. One bright moonlight night a donkey strayed from a village close by, and seeing the deer lying down went to have a closer inspection. After looking at it for a little while he gave a loud bray and this so frightened the deer that he jumped up, pulled the pole away, and thereby brought down the canvas on the top of the commanding officer; he then made a clean bolt of it and was never seen again.

At Attock we crossed the Indus by bridge of boats and encamped close to the river. Quite a scare during the night! For some time the Hindoos had been looking forward with dread to crossing, as they look on the river as accursed. Great therefore was their terror when in the middle of the night we had two shocks from an earthquake: they thought it a judgment on them. I rented a house at Peshawur close to the church, Dr. O'Donnel sharing it with me. From the first I never liked the station, and the severe outbreak of cholera in 1869 did not make it more attractive. The doctor had hard work of it, and we lost many men. Before it broke out a circular had been sent to all the medical men, containing a theory regarding cholera which had been submitted by a German doctor; his idea was that the water underground had something to do with it, and that it would be advisable to watch it rise and fall. Accordingly, a well was selected and set apart for the experiment. A wall was built round it to shut it off, and O'Donnel was put in charge. Every morning and evening he used to visit it. At the side of the well there was a rod with a large float at the bottom to make it buoyant and enable it to rise or fall with the water; by this means he was able to know whether it diminished or increased. One day he came back quite excited, and said he did not know what was going to happen, but there was a difference of one foot in the height since the day before. The cholera, sure enough, did come the next day, but the rise and fall of the water had not much to do with it. It was ascertained that the float had been appropriated by some frogs as a resting-place, and, of course, when half a dozen fat frogs got on board, down it went. It was given up, as, when the cholera did come, we had no time for experiments.

One case was very sad. A young subaltern in

one of the native regiments had a great dread of the epidemic, so much so that his commanding officer sent him on leave into the district to see if he could overcome the feeling. It was of no use. Soon after his return he was seized, and died in two days. His young wife, to whom he had been married but a short time, was also ill in an adjoining room. A Captain Chalmers who was doing duty with us also succumbed. Just before his death, as he was a Roman Catholic, I had to go in the middle of the night and fetch the priest. I did not like him much; he was an Italian, and not very cordial to those of another faith; but he was an energetic old man. He one day showed me his house and church; in the former he had a sewing machine, with which he made his own collars and cuffs. He got grapes from the bazaar and made his own wine, some of which he gave me to taste, and it was really very good, like Sauterne. Vermicelli he also made. He was obliged to do all this, as he said his pay was very small. "If I had the pay your chaplain has!" he remarked to me one day. His congregation made him a present of a very smart pony and trap, of which he was very proud.

We lost a great number of men. The doctors racked their brains to find out the cause, but with no result. By some it was thought that fruit was the cause, and accordingly fruit-sellers were ordered to shut up shop. One who had a stall at the gate leading to the city had a great grievance: he said he had only just laid in a fresh supply, and could not afford to throw it away. All the same he was forbidden to sell it; so he, his wife and children, lived on it for so long as it lasted. They thrived on it too—no cholera for them!

I noticed that sometimes during the time that the epidemic lasted a green mould would appear on the young shoots of shrubs in the garden; also a scum of an oily nature on the surface of the water of the tanks in the lines. Then the men came into hospital, four or five at a time. No cure has as yet been found for this disease, but I have often wondered if anything could be deduced from the blood-poisoning as caused by cholera, and that by the bite of a snake. If I am correct, in the former the blood becomes coagulated, and the patient begs for water to drink, and in the latter the blood becomes liquefied. Is it possible that one poison would annul the effects of the other? The native treatment is to give as much water as the patient can drink. Two cases I have known of recovery, when all remedies had been tried and the case was deemed hopeless, by the patient being allowed to have what he fancied; in one case it was beer, a whole bottle being drunk at a draught; the patient laid his head on the pillow, broke into a gentle perspiration and recovered. In the other case champagne was asked for and given, with the same result. But of course neither of these cases could be taken as a guide to go by.

The Ameer of Cabul, Shere Ali, with a large

retinue came to Peshawur, while we were there, to meet the governor-general. Some of his men were wearing the breast-plate of those regiments which were cut up in the massacre of 1841-42. Among the followers who came with him was a man named Bahadur Khan. He had at the time of the Cabul disaster charge of the English prisoners, and when their release was effected they gave him a certificate, testifying to his civility and attention. This document Mr. Bourk, photographer at Peshawur, made a copy of, and I obtained one from him. It is most interesting, containing, as it does, the names of many well-known men. The Ameer received some valuable presents from Government, among which were guns and elephants; and for all this a heavy toll was levied to go through the Khyber Pass—not even the Ameer's property could go through free. The commissioner entertained the Ameer a good deal, and he made a very close inspection of all that he saw in the house, particularly the knick-knacks that he saw on the drawing-room table. At times his manner was most objectionable. When taken to the house of a bachelor to see how they lived, tea was provided for him. He lifted the cup to his lips, drank some of it, and then spat it out again on the carpet, saying: "You don't call that tea, do you?" The general gave him a parade, and he kept us waiting two hours in full dress, rain falling all the time.

While at Peshawur a singular instance occurred

of native prescience, the truth of which I can vouch for. The station at Nowshera, sixteen miles from Peshawur, was the scene. Before our arrival the garrison there had been increased by the addition of a regiment of cavalry. Three officers, namely, Lieutenant Anderson, Lieutenant Williamson and Dr. Palmer agreed to club together and build one large house instead of three separate ones. When the walls were a few feet above ground, a Mohammedan native officer came and said that they were building their house over where a very holy man had been buried. He did not for a moment suppose that they knew anything about it, but he came to warn them that if they went on and lived in the house when finished they would come to an untimely end. They said that having gone so far they could make no alteration now; and the building went on, was finished and taken possession of. One evening I rode out, intending to go and see how a game of polo was progressing between the Nowshera team and ours. I had not gone far down the Mall before I met four men carrying a native charpoy (a bed), on which was laid a body covered with a cloth; when I asked what was the matter, I was told that the Adjutant Sahib from Nowshera had been killed at polo. This was Lieutenant Anderson, before mentioned. Not long after this a party was out hawking; in the chase two of the riders collided, and one horse, that ridden by Lieutenant Williamson, came down; the rider was picked up dead, his neck being broken. The doctor, the last of the three, was drowned out yachting, near Allahabad, if I remember right. The boat capsized, and he and his companions being good swimmers were making for the shore, joking over the occurrence, when he suddenly went down and was never seen again. On that same day the house was burnt to the ground. All this happened within the year.

After I retired from the service and came home, I told this story at a dinner party, at a friend's house at Norwich, and one of the guests, an army medical officer, said: "I can cap that story with one equally curious. On one occasion a brother officer of mine on his way down the Indus to join his regiment at Kurrachee, stopped to go and see the Muggur Tulao (a place where a number of alligators are kept and fed by the priest). He carried a golail (pellet bow) with him, and amused himself by firing clay pellets at them. Of course no harm was done, as the pellets rebounded off their scales, except in one instance; unfortunately an alligator was struck in the eye, and the eye was completely torn out. The priests were in a terrible rage, and, although my friend offered them any compensation they thought he ought to make, refused to be pacified, and as he went away said: 'In the same way that you have injured this poor beast shall you suffer'. He continued his journey and joined his regiment. A few days after he had to attend at the rifle range, where the company was going through the annual course, and from the marker's butt was watching the shooting, when a bullet striking the iron target splashed, and a fragment rebounded and took out one of his eyes." I think these two stories are very wonderful instances of prognostications coming true. Some to whom I have told them have said that they are mere coincidences, nothing more! That may be, but to me it does not appear a satisfactory explanation.

CHAPTER XIV.

TULLA GAON AND CASHMERE.

Khyberees of the Pass—The chowkedar—"Good and faithful servant"—An eccentric chaplain—My house at Tulla Gaon—A zebra hunt—Transposition of place names—Visit to Cashmere—Discomforts of an ekka—The question of pay—A quarrelsome pony—Horns for sale—From Baramulla by boat—The Maharajah's present—Pedlars' wares—A *Shakara*—Shawls and silks—Crows *v.* snake—View from Takht-i-Suliman—Sacred fish at Bawan—Gul Murg—Back to Srinagar—Fishing, but not for ancestors—A shawl manufactory—Charms of the Cashmere valley.

BEFORE leaving Peshawur, I wished to visit the Khyber Pass; but one could not go alone, nor would it do to go with a military escort; so I wrote to the commissioners to grant me an escort of the Khyberees. It came, composed of wild-looking ruffians, armed to the teeth, with pistols, and those long, formidable knives they are so fond of. They were all part of the tribe that hold the Pass and look upon it as their own, and very jealous are they of their rights. Even with this guard, I was only allowed to go a short distance; but it was far enough for what I wanted, namely, to make a sketch of the scenery about the entrance. On the way back we stopped at Jumrud Fort for a picnic luncheon that we brought with us; and to keep the guard in humour I offered prizes for shooting at a mark—pistols only. It was wonderful what good practice they made, considering their weapons, old cavalry pistols, where obtained, goodness only knows—most likely by robbery, for they are born thieves, and arms are their chief object. Rifles frequently disappeared, in spite of every precaution, and horses, even, they do not hesitate to appropriate if they get the chance.

We all had to entertain a chowkedar (a watchman) while at Peshawur. Not that he personally did much to protect one's goods and chattels, for I believe he was asleep the greater part of the night, but it was a kind of blackmail, he being most probably as great a thief as any of them; his presence, however, was a protection. On one occasion, a chowkedar was on the alert, and the result was fatal. A Mr. Lowenthall, a missionary, was in the habit of walking about his compound on a hot night, and generally lost in thought. One night his chowkedar, not recognising him, challenged him three times, and receiving no answer, fired, unfortunately with too straight an aim, for Mr. Lowenthall fell dead. On his tombstone, after a description of the manner of his death, was inscribed: "Well done, thou good and faithful servant".

We had rather an eccentric chaplain when we first arrived. I have explained before that my house was close to the church. Well, one Sunday, while I was dressing, he rushed into my room in a great state of excitement, and said he had to administer the Sacrament, and had no wine; could I help him in any way? He suggested port wine, but we had none in the mess. I asked if claret would do. No, he would not have that, but asked for a bottle of sherry, and sherry he would have. The last I saw of him, he was running over to the church as fast as he could, a bottle of sherry in one hand, and a cork-screw in the other, and his canonicals flying in the air!

After three years at Peshawur, in 1871 we received orders to go to Tulla Gaon, a small station away in the country between Rawul Pindi and Jhelum. No houses for rent, all had to be bought; mine cost me 2,000 rupees: one large room, bed-room, bath-room, and verandah all round. It had a thatched roof over the ordinary flat one, and I think was cooler than any of the others; I found it very comfortable. In leaving Peshawur I was the only officer with the regiment that had marched in. One had died and the others had gone on leave, three to England, mostly on sick-leave. As the new musketry regulations were just out, the greater part of one's time was spent at the range. The practice at first was not very encouraging, but it gradually improved. The assistant adjutant-general for musketry who paid us a visit was a fine shot himself, a noted shikaree, and the author of a very interesting book on ibex shooting.

He was the hero of a very good story when

with his regiment. At one time a newly joined subaltern made himself obnoxious by the way in which he boasted of what he had done in the shooting line, till at last it was determined to take a rise out of him and put a stop to it. The next time he began he was asked if he had ever shot a zebra; he was obliged to confess that he had not, but would much like to. This they thought could be managed and would let him know when they could take him out. In the meantime a donkey was procured from the bazaar and was painted with black and yellow stripes to resemble a zebra. When ready it was taken to a small jungle and there made fast; and then the anxious sportsman was told that they might start the next day, as khubber (news) of a zebra had been brought in. It was arranged beforehand that he was to have a good trudge before the "game" was approached; so off they started early in the morning, and did not come near the quarry till late in the afternoon; then as they approached the jungle he was told to "look out"; in a little while the "zebra" came into view. Kneeling down and taking aim he fired, and over went the poor donkey. What happened then was quite spontaneous and really the best part of the joke. He said he would like to have the skin, and accordingly it was stripped off. Then looking at the body he asked if it was good to eat. "Oh, well," they said, "that depends; some might like it." It is scarcely credible that there and then he had the hind legs cut off and sent to the general commanding, with his card and compliments. When all became known he was so laughed at that he sent in an application for an exchange. The whole of this was carried out by my friend, the assistant adjutant-general for musketry.

It is very curious how natives will transpose the names of places or stations. For instance, instead of calling it Tulla Gaon, its proper name, many will call it "Gaon Tulla". Lucknow is also called "Nuck Lao," and with English names the same; Ouchtalony is always "Lonyochta". I never could understand why it was done, and I don't believe they could tell themselves.

This year (1873) I carried out an intention that I had long cherished—that of visiting Cashmere. I chose the Murree route, *viâ* Rawul Pindi, as being most convenient and easier in every way; but I had the most uncomfortable journey, before I reached Pindi, that I ever experienced. The way lay across country until one reached the grand trunk road. I could have ridden, and this would have been easier; but then I had some traps I wished to have with me, so I hired an ekka and a driver. This is a one-horse vehicle, used only by natives. The occupant must sit with his knees doubled up to his chin, a most fatiguing position to any one but a native; and, besides this, the hood with which it is provided is so low that one's head is being continually bumped. How thankful I was to reach Pindi! The forty miles between this and Murree were performed in the cart that carries the mails. As the lieutenant-governor of the Punjab also contemplated going to Cashmere, I was warned beforehand that I might have difficulty in obtaining coolies when once within the territory; so having obtained sufficient number to start with, I determined to try and make my service attractive by paying them myself. Their pay is four annas (6d.) each for the march, and generally this is paid by one's servant to the head man of the gang, the consequence being that the unfortunate coolie is heavily mulct. After the march I made them sit down in a ring, went round and dropped a brand new four-anna piece into the hands of each. They were delighted, and the consequence was that they went right through with me to Baramulla (122 miles), and I looked forward to having a good time. I had two ponies, one to ride and the other in charge of my khitmitgar for his pots and pans. This, after I had had an early cup of coffee, I sent on ahead with orders to stop about half-way, or wherever there was a suitable place for a halt, and have tiffin ready. Here I would stay during the afternoon, sketching, and I certainly was not disappointed in its being enjoyable. I was all alone. There were several travellers at Murree who intended going to Cashmere, but their time and mine did not suit, so that for the whole distance the rest-houses were unoccupied, save by myself. They were not very grand buildings: they had no doors and no furniture whatever, and were not so comfortable as my tent; but then by using them I saved my servants the work of pitching it. The pony I had to ride was almost useless in the hills, being unaccustomed to them; and if he saw any other pony on the road he did all he could to get at him and have a fight. On one occasion he caused the death of one. I happened to be riding him at the time along a path on one side of which was a steep precipice and on the other the side of a mountain; suddenly I saw a long string of laden ponies coming towards me, each carrying two large sacks of grain. There was barely room to pass, and the slope was too steep for me to leave the path; so I got off and pushed him as close as I could to the inner side. All managed to pass but one. I suppose his load was larger and projected farther than the others, for as he passed he just touched my pony's quarters. Up to this I had managed to keep him quiet, but this I suppose he looked on as an insult, for he let drive with his hind legs, and the poor baggage pony, load and all, disappeared over the khud (precipice).

On the last march before arriving at Baramulla, I came across men at the road-side with a number of horns for sale—ibex, markhoar, burrul, etc.; I thought what a fine reputation I could establish on my return by the expenditure of a few rupees. Passing this same place on my return, I found that *all the horns had been sold.*

At Baramulla I hired a boat for myself and traps,

and off we started up the river. The boatman, his wife and family occupied a part of the boat at the stern, partitioned off by matting; here also my servants had their quarters, and did the cooking; the boat was tracked up the river, the whole family taking it in turn; at night we made fast to the bank. How enjoyable it was! In three days we reached Srinagar. Here, in a fine grove of chenar trees, I pitched my tent. Soon after, the Maharajah's agent, who had charge of the bungalows erected for visitors, came and offered me one; but I preferred my tent, at all events for the present. He was very civil, and offered to assist me in any way he could. After he had been gone some little time the Maharajah's present arrived, which every new-comer receives, but regulated according to rank. Mine consisted of one sheep, tea, sugar, almonds and raisins, fruit and 150 earthen jars full of sweetmeats! These I gave my servants, and I believe that they lasted them the whole time I was in Cashmere. After this the tent was surrounded by pedlars bringing goods of all kinds for sale: jewellery, silver and copper ware, papier maché, silks, shawls, chogaas and cloth.

The first thing was to hire a boat, called shakara, for the evening airing and excursions; they are manned by six or eight men and are very light; there are no seats; carpets and cushions are laid at the bottom of the boat, on which one reclines, with a back to lean against.

Directly it came I told the boat-man to take me to the best shop for shawls; on arriving the owner came to the steps to receive me, and ushered me into a large room upstairs, full of shawls and cloth goods. Nothing could be done until we had had some tea; this was handed round with small sweet cakes, all very good and nicely served.

Then the inspection commenced; two men came in and proceeded to open out the goods; such shawls and silks! There was a bale of the latter, the most beautiful thing in that way I ever saw; it was very thick and corded; colour, cream-white; and on each side, running the whole length, was a gold tape border about five inches wide. My visit was not for the purpose of buying for myself, but to execute a commission; all the same they were very happy to show me everything.

This boating is a delightful way of getting about, and I was reminded of it when years after I visited Venice.

Whilst sketching an old temple one day I witnessed a very curious sight. From out of the water that surrounded the building came a long black snake, and directly he showed himself, down pounced a number of crows. They seemed to hold a short consultation, and then proceeded to attack; a small number hopped about in front to attract his attention, the remainder attacked him from behind; if he turned round, those in front were down upon him. This went on until they killed him.

Behind the bungalow is situated a hill called Takht-i-Suliman (Throne of Solomon), about 1,000 feet high. On reaching the summit one has a magnificent view of the country around. From there I saw the windings of the river Jhelum which are said to have given the idea for the celebrated cashmere shawl pattern. On the summit is an old Hindoo temple. The Shalimar Gardens on the Dal Lake are very beautiful, and derive great interest from the mention made of them in Lalla Rookh. On the lake one sees the floating gardens on which are cultivated melons and cucumbers.

In June I made an excursion to Bawan where there is a sacred tank full of fish fed by the priests. I was permitted to occupy a room in one of the buildings surrounding the tank, under a promise that during my stay I would not eat beef. The fish are very tame, and come eagerly to the edge for food; some are very large, but they did not look wholesome. From Bawan I went to Gul Murg, a mountain between 2,000 and 3,000 feet high, where most of the visitors congregate when the weather gets hot; on the summit is a plain covered with flowers, and surrounding it on a slight rise is a forest of pines. Directly I arrived my coolies proceeded to cut down trees to build me a hut; this was finished by the evening, as well as a stall for my pony. We had a very good time while there: races, picnics, and parties made up for exploring. The air was perfect. These huts which we all had, being built of pine wood, were not exactly fireproof, and occasionally there was a scare at night from one catching fire; the only thing to be done then was to pull the burning part down, water in sufficient quantity not being available for putting it out.

I stayed at Gul Murg about a month, and then went back to Srinagar as I wished to finish my sketches. This time I occupied one of the bungalows on the bank of the river; it was very comfortable, but destitute of furniture; still, as one lived rent free, one could not complain. Trout was to be had in the river and, strange to say, a mulberry is about as good a bait as any. No fishing is allowed near the Maharajah's palace, for fear you might catch his father or grandfather, as the transmigration of souls is believed in. The boatmen have a strange dread of the river when it rises, and the depth is increased considerably. On one occasion it rose high enough in some places to top the banks, and then I had the greatest difficulty to induce the boatmen to go out. It was very funny to watch the cattle which were grazing about when a sudden gust of wind came; it always brought down a crop of apples off the trees, and then you saw a regular stampede to get to the fruit. The thud of the apples on the ground is heard by them a long way off.

I went to see a shawl manufactory, and a more miserable place for such work I never saw. It was a long shed built of mud, leaking in several places. On each side, extending down the length, were tables at which men and boys worked. Down the centre the space was vacant, and up and down this walked the man in charge reading out the pattern. How miserable the poor creatures looked!—and no wonder, considering that they worked from the time it was daylight till it was dark for the sum of four annas (6d.) a day. Many lose their sight, as the work is most trying to the eyes. It was quite wonderful to see the way in which they blended the different colours together. This is the way those shawls are made for which Cashmere is so celebrated.

The more one sees of the country the more does one vouch for the truth of the saying, "If there be a paradise on earth, it is this! It is this!" For a more lovely spot on earth there can hardly be, nor a more charming place to roam about, with one's tent to pitch in any spot one takes a fancy to, and the people civil and obliging; the stay here spoils one for any other part, and I often thought what a pity it was it did not belong to us. It was with great regret I felt my stay coming to an end; I had enjoyed my trip immensely, and was very glad I had seen the lovely valley.

CHAPTER XV.

HOME AGAIN.

Preparations for the lieutenant-governor—Novel footstools—Evening festivities—Back to Baramulla—Modern improvements—A paradise for artists—Return to Tulla Gaon—Disappointment of an enthusiast—In command of the regiment—The Rev. Geo. Maxwell Gordon—An ill-equipped native convert—Right type of missionary for India—The modern carpenter as Christian teacher—Back to Mooltan—A strange coincidence—Greeting by Bomunjee—Brigadier-General MacPherson relieves Brigadier-General Ross—Recollections of twenty-five years earlier—Pay-day—A steeplechase of jackals—Regrets on leaving—Coonorr—Seringapatam—Famous quarters—Colonel Malleson's description of an historic scene—Colonel Scott's house on the Cauvery—Nundydroog—An eerie resting-place—Rats in force—By bullock-cart—Madras—*The Young Cadet*—The titled barber—A pleasant meeting on the *Trinacria*—White-water—Five ways of getting to India—A dream premonition verified—*L'enfant terrible*—Home again—A farewell.

About this time the arrival of the lieutenant-governor of the Punjab was daily expected, and great preparations were made for his reception. One of the palaces on the left bank of the Jhelum was being got ready for him; and very comfortable they had made it, showing great taste too. The upholstering was all done with Cashmere shawls, and scattered about the floor of the room were small footstools of a design I had never seen before. A shallow wooden box was divided by thin battens, forming different patterns, and the spaces between were filled with mould and then planted with flowers, the colours carrying out the design. Wonderfully pretty they were and very novel. This idea was carried out on a larger scale on the evening of the lieutenant-governor's arrival. In the centre of the river, extending as far as the first bend, were moored floating rafts, divided in the same manner as the footstools, only into much larger designs, and then planted with flowers; round the edge of these rafts were small lamps of different colours, and when they were lighted up at night the effect was very beautiful. All Cashmere turned out that night on the river, I think, for it was crowded with boats; jostling was frequent and the row deafening. The visitors, of whom I was one, were all invited guests of the Maharajah's, and saw it all from the roof of the palace. He gave an evening party, which included a nautch, in honour of the lieutenant-governor's visit.

Well, at last I had to leave, and, as before, by boat to Baramulla. Going with the stream, paddles were used instead of towing, and it was not nearly so pleasant; there was no longer that sound of the rippling at the bows as the boat went through the water which to my idea is so delightful to hear. From all accounts the journey now (1906) is robbed of a great deal of its former charm; roads have been made and improved so that one can drive by tonga (pony cart) all the way, and the Bohemian character that prevailed during my stay in the valley has disappeared; if so, I am glad I went when I did. But still, to any one anxious for a trip where entirely new scenes are desired, I would say, "Go to Cashmere"; I am sure they would never regret it. A charming climate and scenery unsurpassable! I wonder more artists do not make this trip; the subjects they would get I am sure would amply repay them; and to avoid the summer heat of India and the winter cold of England a twelve months' absence should be arranged for.

Several varieties of fruit can be had for the picking, such as apples, grapes, walnuts, mulberries, peaches, cherries, apricots, pomegranates, hazel-nuts and pears. The grapes are particularly fine, and as many as eighteen varieties are to be found. Flowers also are abundant and gorgeous, and the plane tree is common.

We came back to Tulla Gaon all right, and got into harness again. I heard of one thing that amused me much. I have said before that there was a good deal to be desired in the shooting of the regiment in this their first year; but the fact was, the men were tired of it: no sooner had they finished the recruit's course, ninety rounds per man, than they had to begin the annual course. Now the commanding officer was a very good shot, fond of shooting, and he thought he could manage to get better work out of them; so just before I left for Cashmere he said to me: "While you are away,

I shall put one of your companies through myself, and see what I can do". He did not tell me the result himself, but I found out from the returns that C Company, the one he took, was the worst in the whole regiment.

Life at Tulla was not very eventful, there being no one there but ourselves; but it was healthy, and I rather liked the station. In the cold weather of 1874-75 we were ordered to join the camp of exercise at Rawul Pindi, the commanding officer was appointed acting brigadier, and for the time being the command of the regiment devolved upon me. I had only one other officer to assist, Captain Waller, but we got on all right, and altogether had a pleasant time at the camp.

In 1875 the commanding officer retired and went home, and I got the command.

I one day received a letter from the Rev. George Maxwell Gordon, a missionary, residing at Jhelum, saying that he was about to make a tour in this district, and would pass through Tulla Gaon on a date named; would I put him up for a few days? He also said six native converts would accompany him, but they would not trouble me as they would go into the city to stay. Now this Mr. Gordon was one of those who thought that a very humble life, living as the natives, partaking of the same food, rice and chupatties, appealed more to the natives and favoured missionary efforts towards conversion. Accordingly, he walked the whole distance, about eighty miles, by daily marches from ten to twelve miles, putting up in the villages and obtaining what food he could; the consequence being that he arrived at Tulla Gaon looking quite exhausted. He even went so far, although it was the hot weather, as to persist for a long time in doing without a punkah; but I managed to dissuade him from doing this, and by feeding up he soon regained his strength. I will quote an instance to show how worse than useless it is to allow these converts to preach before they thoroughly understand what they are saying. I may mention that one of those converts before named began to preach in the city on the following Sunday. It so happened that he was blind with one eye, and he took for his discourse the words of our Saviour to the messengers of St. John the Baptist: "The blind received their sight". One of the listeners said that he was either a fool or was telling them lies, because, if what he said were true, how was it that he was still blind with one eye? Thereupon the preacher was jeered at and laughed out of the city.

I have always felt very strongly on the necessity of all missionaries sent to India being gentlemen and good theologians. In the first place, the native is an absolute judge of a real "Sahib," and again nothing does more harm to the work of evangelising among natives than for one not to be able thoroughly to explain any complicated questions concerning Christianity.

Mr. Gordon himself was all that could be desired as a missionary, a thorough gentleman, and most unselfish. He never drew any stipend from the society, and lived on his means, the greater part of which he spent in charities. Poor man, he was killed in the Afghan campaign whilst trying to succour the wounded. He went out to a shrine, where he heard there were some wounded, in order to bring them in under a heavy fire, when he was unfortunately struck by a bullet, which went through his wrist and entered his side. He died the same afternoon.

When we were at Allyghur there was a missionary living in the place, a German; he had been a carpenter and was very illiterate, and, as can be imagined, his converts were few and far between; I do not think he did any good whatever. Again, beyond Narkhunda, on the confines of Thibet, there was another of the same class; he had been there fifteen years, and all he had to show for his work was one very halting convert!

Soon after, orders came to go to Mooltan in ordinary course of relief; once more to our station of 1849. I wrote beforehand to a friend there to take a house for me. Now he did not know anything about my having been there before, so that my astonishment was great when I found he had selected the same house that Priestly and I had built twenty-five years earlier. The place was not much altered, but many more houses had been built of course. One of the first to pay me a visit was old Bomunjee, Parsee merchant, with whom I had had dealings before; and he said: "Ah, sir! when you left this, years ago, I said, if you recollect, the next time you come it will be as colonel in command of a regiment; and so it has come to pass!"

Brigadier-General Ross was commanding the brigade when we arrived, but in a few days he was relieved by Brigadier-General MacPherson. The 13th Bengal Lancers were there, and the 92nd Gordon Highlanders, besides a battery of Artillery commanded by Captain Campbell.

Seeing the old house again brought back to my recollection the difficulties Priestly and I had to contend with in providing means for carrying on the building. Some days there would be a full complement of men at work; then it would dwindle down to two or three till funds were once more flourishing. We were each allowed an orderly to superintend the workmen, and I must say they did us right good service; but pay-day was a most uncomfortable time. I can see the old pay havildar (sergeant) now, coming with a bag in his hand (very small) containing balance of pay due. He would then produce his account book, which, as a contrast to the bag of rupees, was very large, and begin to read out that on such and such a date so much was drawn, and so on to the end of the month; and then the balance out of the bag was handed over, and what a short time it took to count that balance! In the meantime anxious applicants were outside waiting to see what they could get. Sometimes they would put a question to the pay havildar as he went out, asking, I suppose, what chance there was for them; a shake of the head was all the satisfaction they got, and if that was not enough they were told the office was closed for the day! It is satisfactory to think that all were paid in the end, and that no one suffered. A house opposite to ours, built by another subaltern, was of a very modest design: one square room, door at each side, verandah all round, with one corner partitioned off for a bath-room.

It was here the occupant one night had a scare. It was a hot night, and he had had his bed placed in the centre of the room with all doors open. Suddenly there was a rush and a stampede, and he felt animals of some kind or other blundering over him; in at one door and out at another they came; it was a pack of jackals in full cry. It turned out that the mess sheep had got out of the pen, and the jackals were pursuing them, running a steeple-chase over his bed.

I left Mooltan in the early part of 1876, having obtained six months' leave, before going to England, in order to see something of the other presidencies, Bombay and Madras.

Before leaving the country for good I must say I was sorry to bid "good-bye". I had been with the regiment fourteen years all but a few months. I liked the native officers and men, and I think I may say without conceit that they liked me. With the European officers I always got on well. They gave me a farewell dinner at the mess, and the next morning came to the station to see me off; I was very glad when the parting was over.

The first place I intended visiting was Coonorr in the Neilgherries; so after reaching Bombay I took my passage in a coasting steamer as far as Beypore, then went by rail to Mettapollium—about the worst place for flies I ever was in; then up the hill to Coonorr by bullock cart, and put up at Grey's Hotel, where everything was clean and comfortable. In the grounds is to be seen the most marvellous heliotrope hedge, fully eight feet high and extending along the whole front of the house; when in bloom the perfume is almost too strong. The scenery round is not grand as in the Himalayas, and the country is more level, but it is very picturesque. In front of the hotel, separated by a valley, is the Droog, one of Tippoo's strongholds.

From Coonorr I travelled to Mysore and visited Seringapatam, most interesting as the scene of one of our early victories in India. I got quarters in the Daulat Bagh and occupied the same room that Colonel Wellesley (Duke of Wellington) had in 1800-1. The walls of the building outside are covered by native paintings depicting a victory of Tippoo's over a small British force that fell into an ambush; the figures are most grotesque. On the left bank of the river one comes to a point where the breach can be seen from the western part of the fortifications, and planted in the ground are still to be seen two guns marking the spot where General Baird issued to storm the fortress. The scene is so beautifully described by Colonel Malleson that I take the liberty of quoting it:—

"The view from this point is striking and impressive; the traveller sees what General Harris, General Baird and Colonel Wellesley saw on that famous morning. The fortress stands now, its guns and defenders excepted, as it stood then. There is the battered fausse-braye and the breached rampart, the ruined cavalier giving no signs of the second rampart below the level of, and separated by a deep ditch from, the rampart which was visible. To the left the enfilading position taken up by the Bombay force, a position which manifestly must paralyse the defence against the direct attack. All is unchanged; there are the stage, the scenery, the footlights; the actors only are wanting."

No one can look on this scene without feelings of admiration for the indomitable pluck that must have been displayed. In the fort there is still to be seen a flagstaff, erected by Colonel Wellesley during the time that he remained at Seringapatam.

On the banks of the Cauvery there is a bungalow that has a very sad story attached to it. It was built by the order of the Rajah of Mysore for Colonel Scott about 1800. He resided there with his wife and two daughters for a few years, till cholera broke out, when his family were attacked and all died. Colonel Scott went to England, leaving all his furniture in the house. The Maharajah directed that nothing was to be moved, and there it has remained all these years. When I went to see it everything of course was in a most dilapidated condition, but it was all just as it had been left.

Nundydroog, another scene of Colonel Wellesley's career, I also visited: a high hill, fortified all round, but having no remains of a citadel, as far as I could see. On the summit is a large house, erected by the late Sir Mark Cubbon, available for travellers. I remained there three days, and a very weird time it was. The wind howled round the house during the night, and, as the doors and windows were somewhat out of repair, it was far from being a comfortable residence. And the rats! I never before saw so many. Night was the time they came out in force, charging across the room like a squadron of cavalry, under my bed and then back again—first one lot and then another—and when I shouted at them they would make a simultaneous rush for the verandah, only to return after a short while. Sleep was almost impossible until the early morning, when they took themselves off. The fort was formerly one of Tippoo's strongholds, where he kept his prisoners, and I was shown a spot at the highest point called "Tippoo's Drop," where they were hurled down below. At certain times of the year looking down one can see the lights of the will-o'-the-wisps flitting about. The natives look upon these as the spirits of the departed. It was a relief to get down below again, for it was cold and dreary up above. No one was there but myself and servants.

Travelling in Madras I found very slow. It did not appear that they had any palki gharries with horses, such as we have in Bengal. I was obliged to have a cart drawn by bullocks, and for an obstinate animal commend me to a bullock; he trots sometimes and sometimes he doesn't, and will often vary the performance by lying down. Then get him up before he chooses, if you can! One's patience is severely tried.

While in Madras itself, I put up at the club, of which I was made an honorary member. Most comfortable it was—considered to be the best in India. An advantage Madras has over the other presidencies is that the houses have such large compounds, with trees, giving plenty of shade. The club compound was like a small park.

The landing now (1906) at Madras, is, I believe, no longer the disagreeable ordeal it used to be. There is a pier for steamers, or, at all events, for boats to go alongside; but formerly one was literally thrown on to the beach, boat and all. The boats used are the most ungainly-looking things possible, very high out of the water, the whole framework lashed together, not a nail in any part of it; but they are the only craft that can go through the surf safely, and they are capitally managed.

Mr. Stevens, in one of his letters from India, is quite right in saying that "Madras is the India of our childhood and our dreams". Neither Bengal nor Bombay come up to what we imagine the country to be; I don't quite know why, but it is so; it may be that most of the books we read when young were about Madras, or written from there. One book I well recollect, *Bishop Heber's Travels*, and another, *The Young Cadet;* the latter had fearful pictures in it, enough almost to deter any one from going to India. One I remember depicted the young cadet of that period waking up in the morning, the first day after his arrival, and seeing a huge snake at the foot of his bed, glaring at him, while the floor of his room swarmed with centipedes, scorpions and all kinds of horrible creatures, and the artist had taken good care not to draw them *too small.* A friend (?) sent me this book soon after I got my cadetship! I forget now if I thanked him for it; I hope I did.

What amusing fellows the barbers are! They all seem to have been presented with silver soap-boxes from celebrities who visited the country, and these they show with great pride. They are not too modest in speaking of themselves. The one who came to cut my hair called himself "King Tom" (the illustrious hair-cutter). This was why, I suppose, he charged one rupee for the operation. I told my servant next time to bring a barber that had not got a title.

I left Madras for Bombay on the 25th of August, and on going on board the *Trinacria*, on which I had taken a passage home, I was very glad to meet Macnaughten, 13th Bengal Lancers, who was also going home with his wife and family; it was as pleasant as it was unexpected. We sailed September 6th, within four days of the date on which I left England on my first voyage; and now this was my last, and I was real sorry to leave. During the thirty years I have been at home I have travelled over the continent and several places in England, and I found out that there are far worse places to live in than India.

Soon after getting out to sea we witnessed that strange appearance which is, I believe, called white-water. The sea all round was white like milk, and the sky being quite black the effect was weird and extraordinary. The captain had never seen it before, nor heard of it, but I had read a description of it in a book, *The Green Hand*, a nautical novel; and also of "the Ripples" which we experienced on the voyage to China. The voyage was not eventful—the usual routine; but going through the Suez Canal was a novelty to me, and completed the series of the different ways in which I had accomplished the voyage, *viz.*, round the Cape in a sailing vessel, round the Cape in a steamer, over-land crossing the desert by horse vans, crossing the desert by rail, and now by the canal, this last the most comfortable of all.

A rather remarkable instance of a dream being

realised occurred. MacNaughten's children had a separate cabin next to his, and one morning he heard one of them crying. Going in to see what was the matter, he found the eldest, Frank, a boy about seven or eight, in great distress; on his father asking him why he cried, the boy said: "O Papa, I have had such a bad dream, and it has frightened me. I dreamt that a large vessel came and ran against our ship, striking her outside just where my bed is, and she did us so much harm." This is exactly as the boy put it. Well, his father quieted him, and all went to rest again. A week after this we went into Gibraltar; there were several vessels there, and one coming out collided with us, striking us, strange to say, in the very spot the boy had described, knocked our boats to pieces on the starboard side and brought down some of our top hamper. His father had forgotten all about it until I reminded him.

A story of a boy on board this same vessel on another voyage was told me, as a good instance of *l'enfant terrible!* One day a lady was talking to one of the passengers, and this boy would come close up to her, rubbing against her dress; she told him to go away, twice, and when he did it the third time she pushed him aside with her sunshade, saying: "Do go away, little boy". He looked at her very sulkily for an instant, and then went below, got hold of the biscuit basket, and then came on deck; again he went up to this lady and annoyed her, and when she drove him off, blew the chewed biscuit he had in his mouth all over her. The gentleman she was talking to took him down below and gave him what he deserved, but the little brute was not done with yet. He watched his opportunity, and in the afternoon, while his corrector was leaning over the rail, looking out to sea, he whipped out an iron belaying-pin, came behind, and with all his force struck him behind the knees, bringing him down, of course, like a shot. What became of the young ruffian after this last effort history telleth not. He ought to have been dropped overboard, I think!

On the 11th of October we arrived at Liverpool, a true English day to greet us, cold, foggy, dreary-looking to a degree!

October 13th I reached home, and met my dear mother again, after seventeen years' absence.

> Yes, we have met, and Home has a spell,
> Though I've loved the land of my sojourn well.
> The work is over, the sojourn done
> Fare thee well, thou Land of the Sun!
>
> Nothing but rest, and home, in store;
> Never again to wander more;
> Thanking God for the PRESENT, and yet
> Linked to the PAST with a fond regret.
>
> ALIPH CHEEM.

"BON SOIR, LA COMPAGNIE."

Good-night! I am old, and my blood has grown cold,
I am weary of banquet and ball;
I have shared of your best, I would go to my rest,
Good-night to you, gentlemen all!

From the laughter and light, I must ride through the night,
Alone from your festival hall;
Looking back through the years with no tremors or fears,
Good-night to you, gentlemen all!

Spur at heel, sword at side, as a man I will ride
With no dolorous trappings or pall,
No tolling of bell, but a smile for farewell—
Good-night to you, gentlemen all!

Fair ladies, adieu! my obeisance to you;
One kiss, lightly blown, to recall
The hey-day of life with its love and its strife—
Fair ladies, Good-night to you all!

The Recorder from whom no man's secrets are hid
Has called me; I go at his call.
I am ready to answer for all that I did—
Good-night to you, gentlemen all!

Good-night! then Good-night! Though your fires burn bright,
With your lustres ablaze on the wall,
Yet the stars are agleam on the ford at the stream—
Good-night to you, gentlemen all!

A. (PIONEER).